Copyright © 2016

Bethune Publishing – The Bethune Group

Anthony "Tony" Thompson

a/k/a Tony Thompson

First Printing

All rights reserved, including the right to reproduce this work in any form whatsoever without written permission from the publisher, except for brief passages in connection with a review. Photographs may not be reproduced without permission of the owner.
For information write:
Bethune Publishing, Inc.
P. O. Box 2008
Daytona Beach, FL 32115-2008
docbethune@tbginc.org

Jacket designed by **John-Mark McLeod**

J2maginations, LLC

J2maginations@gmail.com

Book design and page layout by
Bethune Publishing, Inc.
Printed in the United States of America

Library of Congress Control Number: 2016921277
ISBN:978-1946566003

In His Arms

Written by
Tony Thompson

Published by Bethune Publishing
Daytona Beach, FL

Table of Contents

Content	Page #
FORWARD	1
DEDICATION	4
SPECIAL GRATITUDE	6
CHAPTER 1	8
CHAPTER 2	23
CHAPTER 3	38
CHAPTER 4	50
CHAPTER 5	73
CHAPTER 6	85
CHAPTER 7	110
CHAPTER 8	129
CHAPTER 9	138
FIRE	153
UNITED STATES AIR FORCE	157
FRIENDS & FAMILY	160

Forward by
Dr. Evelyn Bethune

I love the telling of family histories and events that helped to shape communities. That is what I find engaging about "In His Arms". Tony Thompson has captured events in his life and connected them to other points in history that give an intimate view of African American life in the north and south. All too often we miss opportunities to tell our stories and how we fit into the very fabric of American History.

In His Arms is a glimpse of real life. Not a perfect life but a life filled with ups and downs, good and bad, fun and family. It is about the coming of age of a Black man in America. The accomplishments of Tony Thompson as historic and yet not unusual for Black America. Though not talked about nearly enough, the everyday happenings in Black communities across America were and are filled with "firsts". Our communities "back in the day" were filled with over achievers who didn't feel like they were doing anything more than upholding the standards of excellence that they were raised by. Education was cherished and respect was given. Bad behavior was not rewarded and second chances were earned.

"In His Arms" tells the story of a man who decided that he was not going to fail and that he was going to do for his children what his father did not do for him. He was unwilling to give up or give in to the racism and discriminatory acts perpetrated against a race of people. Because he excelled, he set an example for those around him, his children and the children he encountered in the system.

This book is a prime example of why it is critical for us to tell our own stories from our own perspective so that generations coming after us will know that we did something. They will know that we did not just go silently into the night but that we fought the good fight, winning many battles. That knowledge will help them to stand in the face of difficulty and be unafraid of adversaries who might appear to be stronger. Knowledge of self and a clear understanding that God never fails helps to level the playing field.

Tony Thompson is a great writer and an even better story teller but best of all, he is an incredible human being with a caring heart and a spirit of determination. This is his first book but I am sure it will not be his last.

DEDICATION

Mom, I dedicate this first book to you because much of it is about you. From my childhood, I shared your joy as well as your pain. I knew you when you were in love with being a mother as well as being a mother of 6 children. You almost always worked 2 jobs. Somehow you made it through and so…this one is for you.

THANK YOU

Dr. Gwen Sanford, (my first cousin): With a strong arm, you made corrections to my work and shared your opinions. I could really hear you from time to time while working on *In His Arms* saying, I didn't know this or that…yet always encouraging me to keep moving forward.

To my siblings: Carl A. Thompson, Altamease Lucas, Debra Sawyer, Brenda Brown and Regina Thompson

To my children: Tony, Jr., Malcolm, Jonathan, Sherri, Marcus, and a host of cousins and other family members

SPECIAL GRATITUDE

To Vickey McCaskill, a very special person in my life, thank you for sometimes sacrificing your time to help make this project a success. I am grateful for your love and strength. Your insights on what would make a smoother flow in my story line helped me to stay the course. Your knowledge of MS Word software brought me out of the stone ages. You will always be close to my heart.

CHAPTER: 1

Although it may be difficult telling you who I am; I can tell you from whom I came. I was born into a household with a mom and dad. My mom, Carrie Mae was a short, beautiful lady with long curly hair. My dad, Carol (pronounced Carl) Love was tall, dark and handsome and had curly hair also. I was born at home on July 4th 1953; downstairs on a sofa in Bailey Heights. It was a very hot day in Waycross, Ga. Of course, I didn't remember this event, but the way it was told to me; I can envision the moment. I would later find out that Bailey Heights was a well-known area housing project in the early fifties. Most of the people that lived there were my cousins, aunts, or friends. I had a brother, Andrew who was five and a sister, Altomease, who was about four, when the family welcomed me as the new baby into the household.

I was named by my first cousin, Blanche. Family members have said that when I was born, I was the spitting image of my grandfather, Papa John Thompson. Now Papa John was a mix of Black and Cherokee Indian. He had hair that hung to his shoulders, and a long, hooked nose. I was told that in his younger days, he was the gleam in a lot of women's eyes. Even in his old age, lots of women; young and old were crazy about some Papa John. He was an average person, by all means, but he appeared to love life. He was always smiling, always happy and never complaining about anything or anyone. Papa John was nice to everyone, with a kind word to share all the time. He was my father's father. Even though it was said that he was a ladies' man, he was always the perfect gentleman.

When I was born, I was described as having curly, black, silky hair, and was bright in complexion. Many would say, "Now that Papa John there", referring to my much-loved grandfather. But as I got a little older, everything about my appearance began to change. I was no longer bright in complexion, my hair no longer curly, black, and silky and all references to me "looking like him", became a memory.

I must have been about 2 years of age or slightly older when I can recall my earliest memories of my grandfather. As a child, I remember a lot of wonderful times. He was a great old man and loved walking wherever he went. I loved walking with him because he was greatly respected. I took pride in saying that's my grandpa. His distinct laughter and huge amplified voice sounded sort of like Santa Clause and brought happiness to those around him.

Whenever he visited any of the relatives, we would meet over to that particular family member's house. Everyone would always prepare to have a big dinner together and anxiously wait for him to sit around and tell us stories about his parents and siblings and the things they went through as a family. Papa John was already an old man at somewhere around 73 to 74 years of age when I was born.

I remember once when he was visiting my mom and dad, the whole family was sitting in the living room talking and having fun. My mother was washing clothes in one of those old, round washing machines with the roller to squeeze the clothes. I was told several times to stay away from that washing machine. They told me that I might get my hand stuck so, don't touch! Even though I understood what I was being told, in my mind, I knew that I could put the clothes through that ringer better than any adult could. It looked so easy, and I had to see that machine squeeze those clothes. I put a rag in the machine and it pulled it through and without warning, pulled my hand and arm with it. I began screaming to the top of my voice. My parents ran into the kitchen, finding me stuck in the wash machine and scared to death. After a few minutes of disassembling the machine, they pulled my arm out and looked me over. After realizing I had nothing broken, they relaxed from the excitement. From then on, this incident made a great addition to my grandfather's collection of stories for when the family came together. It was also at this point that I inherited a new name of, "Mr. Tony".

Between the ages of 2 to 3, I was no longer the baby. I now had a little sister and her name was Debra. My father used to call her "his little black angel" and he said she looked like his mother, (she had long, silky hair too) and was a beautiful black baby with curly hair that she would keep through adulthood.

My grandpa was over for one of his regular visits and my baby sister was in the bed sleep. I found a box of matches (the kind you can strike on the wall or floor). I had seen my father and mother use them enough, so I figured I knew how to use them as well. Well, I got one lit and now I had to find something to burn. The bed spread looked like the thing to try. So, I put the lit match to the spread and it began to burn; putting out a beautiful glow. It began to get hot and I couldn't put it out. I ran into the living room to get my parents, screaming that the bed was on fire. Part of my panic, of course, was due to the fact that my baby sister was still in the bed, and I was worried about her also. They managed to get the fire out and my baby sister was not touched. As high as the flames were, it was a miracle that she didn't get burned. Of course, "Mr. Tony" was in trouble again and knew not to play with matches anymore or at least for a little while. I had a very hard head and it wasn't long before I was getting into trouble again. I was a very curious child and loved to experiment with things that I really didn't understand but, of course, thought that I did. They probably should have called me "Mr. Know-It-All."

Now I don't know if someone told my sister about the fire because when she got older, she couldn't stand me when we were growing up. We were always arguing and fighting about something.

With the two major incidents of the washing machine and the fire to my credit; whenever anything happened in the house, everyone would be like "Tony did it", and most of the time, I did. But there were times that I really didn't do it, and the fact that no one believed me really hurt.

Well, the family kept growing and along came Brenda, another sister and more help for Debra. A few years later, yet another sister by the name of Regina would be added to the brood. Along with my oldest brother Andrew, my older sister, Altomease, there were a total of six kids: four girls and two boys. The boys were outnumbered. Now we were a family of eight and as my brother got older, he didn't have much time for me. When he left the house, I was really outnumbered! Anything I did, Debra would tell my big sister, Altomease, and you know what happened? Yep, I got a beat down! I tried to fight back, but my big sister was good with the "windmill", so I didn't stand a chance. And then after she would beat me down, she would put me out of the house. Anyone that had a big sister like mine knows exactly where I'm coming from.

In the absence of my brother, I knew I had to find some buddies to hang out with. I learned to find my way around the neighborhood and was everywhere. I had my own group of little friends, and my mother would say, "Look at you thinking that you a lil man, bossing your friends around". It came easy telling my friends what to do, like: Collecting pop bottles, raking people's yards, and doing anything to make money. Those were the days when you could buy a bottle of soda pop and 10 cookies for 10 cents. The corner store was one of our favorite places to hang out.

One of my greatest joys of being outside of the house was running around barefoot. Now that was total freedom. Even though I may have been the boss in the streets, when I got home I had to deal with my big sister. She would say, "You may tell those lil' piss tail boys what to do, but when you home, you do what I tell you to do!" When my brother was home, he kept her off me. But as soon as he left the house, it was on again. She would say, "Now that your brother's not here run your mouth now!" I learned very quickly when to turn my mouth off and when to keep my mouth shut.

One day, I found my way over to my grandfather Papa John's house. By this time, he was in his 80s and I was about 7 years old. He would always offer me something to eat and it would always be grits and eggs. I asked him one day why was that the only thing he ate, and he replied; "It was easy to cook and easy to digest". I accepted that answer, and would always go by and check on him, only occasionally eating grits and eggs. Papa John was the type of man that loved to move. I would go by and he would be packing up to move again. I would ride on the back of the truck to his new place, help him set up his new house, and a few months (six to seven), he would be moving again. He was like a nomad, packing up his tent and going off to a new adventure.

I loved being around Papa John. Being born around 1880, he would tell me stories about his life and the things that he experienced. In passing those stories down to me, he would say, "Mr. Tony, I have plenty grandchildren, but you are the only one that will come and spend time with me." Some of my first cousins were adults in their 20s. He would say, "I don't know about those other boys, but you are going to be somebody". I think he said that because the other boys were too busy chasing girls.

My grandpa lived during a time when education was not a priority in his family. He would send off for materials as basic as the ABC's and other reading material and taught himself to read. Everywhere he went, if he saw a sign, he would read it. Whether he was riding or walking, he would read the signs out loud. Papa John was a proud man and a ladies' man. Whenever he would pass by a lady, no matter her color, how old, or how she looked, he would take his hat off to her. He was well respected because of the way he carried himself. In the late 50s and early 60s, during the time of segregation, there was a white side of town and a black (or colored) side of town. Signs that said "colored" meant that you were to use the back door. There were white and black water fountains, as well as white and black movie theaters. No matter how old a black man was, they would be greeted with a "Hey boy", even by the little white children.

My grandpa was about 6 feet 2 inches, and a very humble man. He told me about the time when he was young and the KKK was after him and killed his sister. He said he never forgot that, but refused to be afraid for the rest of his life. Everywhere he went, he went with a bible in his hand and wearing a nice suit. Now where ever he lived he would plant a garden. He loved fixing and repairing things.

There was this old man that noticed me always helping my grandpa John so he would ask me to do little things for him like, go to the store or other little jobs. I had a little running buddy, and one day, we needed some money, so we went by the old man's house. The man was about blind and could not walk; he had no legs and was confined to a wheelchair. On top of that he couldn't count. He gave me a $5 bill and told me to get something that cost about a dollar. Just like any other times, he trusted me to count his money. When I gave him his change back, I didn't give him all his money. He kept asking, "Don't you owe me more money?" I said, "No." keeping three dollars in my pocket. He got angry for the first time, saying "You are a god damn lie". That day, I lost a good friend in that old man. He always gave me something for helping him. Life lesson: He lost trust in me and the old guy really liked me. He told my parents and from then on, I had to let them know where I was going, at all times. I stayed in hot water for a while, but I was still sneaking around doing things that I had no business doing like climbing over barbwire fences and stealing pecans off pecan trees. Or I was in other people's yards, raiding their plum trees. I kept a pole with a net on the end to catch the plums. Me and my buddies went one day for pecans and my pants got caught on the fence. It tore my pants off me and I had to walk all the way home in my underwear. Of course, it seemed like everybody was outside that day, laughing and pointing. It took me a while to live that down, because everyone kept reminding me.

With my ability to find trouble, this one particular day would be no different. One day when both of my parents were at work, my first cousin Irene was babysitting us. My parents had told me whatever you do, don't go across the street. They are burning timber and a lot of tar was flying off the wood and it was very hot. I had to go over anyway and climb up and down the trees, and jump across them with the rest of the kids. Until all of a sudden I heard a loud popping and cracking sound and then something hot hit me in the center of my back. After this happened several times, I ran home screaming. When I got to the door of the house, I was moaning and in pain but I didn't say a word. I went straight upstairs and got into bed. When my parents got home they wanted to know where I was. I'm not quite sure how they found out but they said "We won't give you a whipping this time after examining your back. God has already done it because you disobeyed your parents. Let that be a lesson to you Mr. Tony." Believe me it was a lesson learned. If you never been burned by hot tar, trust me... you don't want to. It's like being on fire and nothing will put it out, water or anything else will not help it. If this is an indication of how hot hell is I knew I didn't want any parts of it. Staying true to form, anything missing or anything that happened, it was Tony that had done it.

We stayed in Bailey heights for quite some time. I got in my first fight that was egged on by some of the older boys. The kid I was fighting was a lot bigger than me and always bullied me. In plain language I was afraid of him, but I didn't let him know that. The fight was on and I guess by luck my first swing hit him in the nose. He broke into a loud cry, crying like a baby. It was my first fight and I won it! I never had problems out of this kid again. As a matter of fact, I got even more friends as a result of that fight. I was the top dog among my friends and the older boys bragged about me for a little while.

We would later move to another side of town. We stayed in this small subdivision called 0-9. My dad bought us two puppies, a male Boxer, and male German Shepherd. The Shepherd, we named King. When he was a puppy, he was very greedy. One day, he ate a piece of chicken and swallowed the whole thing, bones and all. A few days later, my Dad noticed he was crying a lot and scrapping his butt on the grown. That dog would cry all night. My dad finally realized that it was something stuck in the dog's butt. He tried first giving the dog castor oil and that didn't work. After examining the dog, he noticed what looked like a bone stuck in his butt. So, my dad had to stick his hand up the dog's butt and remove the bone. From that day on, that was one mean dog. He wouldn't let anyone around the kids and if anyone of the kids got a whipping, my dad would have to close the door. King would try to attack my dad, so my dad would say that that dog is crazy. He would say, "I feed you and you gon' try and bite me?!" People would walk by our house but knew not to come in the yard.

There was this bad alcoholic in the neighborhood name Mr. Abraham. He would pass by our house to go to the store but was afraid of King and always complained about him. One morning about a year or so after we moved, all the kids were getting ready for school. King was lying in the front yard foaming out of the mouth. The first person we thought of was Mr. Abraham. King had been poisoned or given food with glass chopped up in it. That was a sad day for all the kids. King was a great protector for the children in my family. He had my dad afraid to beat us. Time passed and Mr. Abraham use to come over our house quite often to borrow rubbing alcohol saying, "My back hurt me so bad". One day, he came over asking for more rubbing alcohol. He stood in front of my mother and her children and drank the whole bottle of alcohol, then asked one of the children to get him a glass of water. I guess it had to be about a week a so later that they found him at home dead. We suspect that it was alcohol poisoning. Our suspicions would be confirmed when people started talking, saying that Mr. Abraham borrowed alcohol for his back from most of the neighbors. Time went on.

Chapter 2

On occasion, my mom would get in the car and take all the children, all six of us to her dad's house in Rebecca, Georgia. And my dad would stay behind. I found out later that this was the times they would be arguing about something. During this time my grandpa Charlie stayed in an old wooden house that sat high on blocks. I remember going to the back door and seeing my mom put clothes in a big black pot full of hot boiling water. It had wood burning underneath it. Out of disbelief I ran to my brother very excited saying, Andrew, Andrew come here quick mama is out here cooking clothes. I had never seen that before.

But those was some of the cleanest and whitest clothes I had ever seen. I couldn't wait to get back home to tell my friends about my mom cooking clothes. Everybody got a big kick out of it and thought it was funny. He stayed just outside of Lumber City, Georgia at the time. The one thing that I remember about being at my grandpa house is he didn't have a T.V. or radio and my mom use to tell us old stories about her growing up. She was a tomboy and loved climbing trees. She told us stories about seeing ghost at night while walking down those old dirt roads in the middle of the woods and other scary moments. After listening to all the stories, we would cuddle up together.

One night, we all was in bed, and it was a big lighting storm. Lighting struck and it sound like it hit the house. My grandfather look outside and the lighting had struck a pine tree right beside the house and the tree was on fire. I think everyone wished they was home. My mom and dad must have made up. We went back home or my grandfather must have got tired of us.

I remember getting home and my mother and father having little house parties on occasions. I had a first cousin that was old enough to be my mother, named Irene, and her husband's name was Wil, Wil was about 6'5" and a very big man and was a career soldicr. Well, this particular day or night, my parents had a coming home party for Wil over our house. One of my father friends got drunk off the moonshine that they would always drank and began to talk crazy out of his head. Wil warned him to calm down once or twice and told him that he would help him out if he didn't behave. I guess the man didn't believe him and continued to act out.

Wil grab the man, put him over his shoulder, took him all the way upstairs, threw him in the tub and turned on the hot water on him, with all his clothes on. He would not let the man get out of the tub until he said he was sober and would not act out again. It wasn't too many of my dad friends that came over from then on. It got crazy around our house.

A few years later, we were headed to my Granddad's house again. My mother's father, at the time, he stayed outside of a little small town named "Rebecca, Georgia." It was in the middle of nowhere. I knew this was not the same house we went to when I was younger and I was sort of disappointed. My granddad lived 3 to 4 miles in the woods and the nearest house to him was about a mile. No lights at night and most of them stayed in log cabin houses with no lights. The cabins had wooden shutters with no glass windows.

My granddad had a water well on his back porch that you had to rope the bucket down to get water. It was always nice and cold when you pulled it up. He had a wood stove that he cooked his food on. The best food I ever tasted. My mother's father was truly a throw back in time. The outhouse was about 30 to 40 feet away from the house out in the woods. At night, he had a pee pot and if you had to number two, you had to go out back to the "out house" at night. At night in the summer, you had to leave the shutters open.

It worried me that he would leave them open at night in fear of wild animals. He had a neighbor down the street that made some good blueberry pies and always made some for my parents whenever we came to visit. He would have the pies sitting in the window and you could smell them from a distance down the road. Now my granddad (mom's dad) had a girlfriend that stayed in town. She had this little jungle so to speak that had all kind of animals, swings and rides like I had never seen. This little place had toys and many other little items that not only me but my whole family was amused by, even my parents. Whenever my mom would visit her she would give her several items to take back home with her. That is where I wanted to be for some reason, I guess I thought I could really enjoy life being at her place. Well, when it was time to go back home to Waycross I didn't want to leave. I didn't want to stay with my granddad; I wanted to stay with his girlfriend.

So, after begging and pleading my parent agreed to let me stay. That was okay. with me that way I would be close to his girlfriend's house. So, he enrolled me into school. I didn't know until he made his first speech who my grandpa Charlie Pace was. I always thought my Granddad was a quiet and humble man. My mom use to say you don't know him like I do. I found out that he didn't play. She was right. I didn't know him like she did. He set down the rules for me. The first one is don't never let me beat you home. Next one was you will work around the house. And when you are out of school on weekends you will go to work with me. If you have to use the toilet at night, you will go to the outhouse. I was put in charge of emptying the pee pot, and it was used for just peeing. When he talked, I just listened. So, whatever I had to do, I made sure I did it before dark. I remember one night, I didn't empty the pee pot and it was dark. He told me he didn't care how dark it was I better get my "you know" out and go empty it. Scared to death, I went to the outhouse and emptied it in pitch black darkness.

On the weekends, I went to work with him picking peanuts. He would say, "Boy don't let me catch you, I'll put this peanut vine on your behind". I knew he would, so I made sure that he never caught me. I was scared to ask him to go over to his girlfriend's house; the main reason I wanted to stay. I kind of left that alone. It wasn't long before I was ready to go home, but I knew not to tell him. I was 7 going on 8 and when he had to tell me something more than one time I got my butt whipped. He did not believe in sparing the rod. I got quite a few whippings staying with him. When I went to school I had to walk about a mile to the next house to be picked up by the bus.

Sometime my grandpa would let me go to that house and play. There were two young boys about my age living there. Most of the time, I had to fight them every day on the way home from school on the bus, and when I was at their house playing. Sometimes it was hard to tell whether they were friends or enemies. One morning, my grandpa told me, "Boy don't let me beat you home today". So, I was up the road and could see my grandpa from miles away coming home so I continued playing and fighting with the boys. They had cherry bombs and was lightening them and threw them at me. So, I decided to go home and was happy knowing that I had beat my granddad home, but when I got there he was already there and steaming. He couldn't find nothing to whip me with so he pulled a rod off the wall. Well you know, he took care of business. I found out later that it was a back way to the house that I knew nothing about. I think that maybe he had planned this, so he would have a reason to kick my butt. I didn't take chances again. I knew better and was at home way before I had to be. Even when my grandpa laughed, he looked mean. I don't know why I didn't notice this before.

One time, my Grandpa Charlie went out with one of his girlfriends and left me with his girlfriend's mother. This old lady must have been 90 plus years old. It was late night and I was sleepy but afraid to close my eyes. I dozed off a couple times and the room seemed to be pulsating back and forth. The old lady asked me if I wanted to go lay in the bed, I politely said "No". I feared her grabbing me. I stayed awake until my grandpa came back to get me.

Now when school was out, I worked with my Grandpa Charlie in the cotton fields, picking "cotton". Again, his motto was, boy if I catch you, I will tear –your ass up. Again, I didn't let him catch me. And he would say, "And make sure you clean them vines", and I did. That December my mother and father came to visit and was bringing me new clothes to wear when school started back. I begged them to let me come home, I didn't want no part of that old man. They even had brought my pellet gun with them again. I pleaded to come home. So, when I was sure I was going home. I went out back with my pellet gun. I had a score to settle. I got as close as I could with my gun and waited on the two boys and their granddad to come out and dig sweet potatoes out of their garden in the back yard. So eventually, they came out. Every time one would bend down to dig, I would shoot one in the butt with my gun. I knew when I hit one; they would raise up and look around. Mission was accomplished and I was ready to go home. In a lot of ways, I was like my grandpa Charlie. I didn't take nothing off anybody if I could help it.

When I got home I felt different about my family including my sisters, yes, and my sister too. I noticed things had change somehow. My dad's two sisters Aunt Lois and Ruby was moving to Florida. My cousin who we called "Brother or Bra Shake" was getting in and out of trouble in gang wars. One side of town again the other. They would make "Zip guns" out of wood a piece of bicycle inner tube and a nail. They would shoot 22 bullets.

Another cousin was fighting in this gang, me and my brother was going to get a haircut and one of the other guys shot his eye out with a bow and arrow We watched as his eye sank into the ground. That was really weird seeing his eye being absorbed into the ground.

Early one Saturday morning I found out that my mother and father had been arguing and fighting for the first time that I had known of and I was confused. My brother and my first cousin "Bro". (My dad's sister's son) went looking for my dad to beat him up. This was another first. Well needless to say, that was the last time my dad and mom lived together as a family. We never stopped loving my father until this day I love my father just like the rest of my sisters and my brother. Even my mother never stopped loving my father. We were a family of 8. We didn't have a lot but we had each other and even though I argued with my sisters I love them. I never realized we were poor. We had just as much as most of the people that I knew and we were happy.

It was so hard to understand why my father left. I think my family waited every day, for quite some time... waiting for my dad to come home. It didn't happen. One day he came by after several months passed, and it was only to say goodbye. He was leaving town.

He said when he got settled he would get in contact with us and send us money to help the family. That never happened. The rest of the family stayed on in Waycross on Butler St. The house we stayed in was an old wooden house high on blocks. There was this big bowl full of military ammo rounds, M16 and bigger. We would build a fire out back and burn the leaves, and throw the bullets into the fire and watch them go off. God was with us we never got shot. These was the time when you could go to sleep with your front door open all night.

Eventually we moved back into the project so my mom had to get a second job, she worked at the hospital and when she got off she went to work as a house (a maid). My mother worked and saved up enough money to buy a car for the family it was a "Green and White 55 Buick. It was a neat car but when you drove it over 50 miles an hour it would rock side to side. My mother had this friend that worked for this white family, her name was Cora. She would come and stay with us sometimes. She was a live-in maid and she was the greatest cook I think I ever saw. She made the best biscuits. The family she worked for and lived with would send us boxes of clothes when she came to stay or visit with up. This was a great help for the family. It had gotten to the point that sometimes I would not have a pair of socks that didn't have holes in them, and I had to wear them to school. The first person that would notice and say something about them would be my first cousin Barbara. You could see the back of my heels.

My brother would go out and work in the tobacco fields. They said I couldn't go because I was too young. So, I stayed home and learned to get alone with my sisters. My Papa John didn't stop coming by, he was still Papa John. He would say "that son of mine". He wouldn't say much but we knew he loved my family including my mother. And I knew everyone loved him. I know that my family was hurting just as much as I was. Every time I saw a man that looked anything like my father I had to make sure, hoping that my dad had come back home. Sometimes I would ask them if they knew my dad.

My mother and father had been together about fifteen years. They met in Newark New Jersey where my oldest brother was born and they were married and moved to Waycross, Georgia. We found out later that he had moved back to Newark. My mother lost her younger brother who had just gotten out of the military and had a lot of women. Mother said some man found him in a Pool hall and shot him to death. My father had just gotten out of the military too. I think it was in 1942.

I found out, years later, the reason we moved back into the projects was because of some kind of a problem between my stepfather and the land lord. We were told we had to move. I had planted a bag of corn in a field next to the house and it had started to grow. It was a nice size area of corn. I had to let go of my first garden.

I had a chance to spend time with both of my grandfathers and I think it was a combination of both of their wisdom that took me through what I was about to encounter. Papa John love and humbleness, and Grandpa Charlie no nonsense attitude, made me responsible for my actions. I didn't know then but making decisions at critical moments would save me and my family life. With my world changing fast around me I had to learn to think like a man. I am sure my brother felt a greater pressure than me. He was the oldest child, only 12 years of age, and I was seven. He had to be the man of the family. My oldest sister, Mease, age 11, had to step it up and take care of the house and my younger sisters. We knew if we were to survive, we had to work together. My mother had this long talk with all of her children. We didn't want to have nothing to do with Welfare. Somehow or another we did on occasions manage to get some of that welfare cheese from one of her friends. I think at times she would get some of that food from one of my aunts. We still had a lot of family at the time in Waycross and we didn't really want for nothing. My mother was just tired of not having nothing and wanted to make a change in our life. I think like all of us she wanted my father to be a man and work with us as a family and have something together. We were growing to know that was just that a wish. Everybody was trying to do their part but it was a slow process. We as a family began to understand how some others felt, that was less fortunate than us. It was very different having a single parent and she's never at home have to work two jobs to take care of the family. When she come home she can't spent time with us, come home and go to sleep. Being home at night by ourselves, well you know that a lot of things went on while she was at work that she didn't know about. When we were supposed to be in the house we were up the streets. When my mother was at home at night we were in the house when it turned dark. Yes, every-thing was changing. I think a little too much too fast. We were not the only children around with a single parent. A lot of them hung out in the streets at night, some of my brother friend would start coming by at night. We know if my mom ever found out we would be in big trouble. Believe it or not girls would be out at night as well and into everything. I plead the fifth on some of the things they would be doing. I think my mom knew that we were getting a little out of control. You know how most moms are they won't say anything they will just catch you in the act and then tear your behind up. That is if she was like my mom. Even though my dad beat us when he was home it wasn't that much.

My mom was normally the one that did the beatings. She didn't play she would make us get our own switch, and if it wasn't a good one she would go get one that she knew you wouldn't like. She would talk to you while she beat you. A cut for every word she said. You prayed that she didn't have much to say. Nobody ran from my mom, we learned early on that she would wake you up whipping you in your draws half asleep.

CHAPTER 3

Over time my mother had to move on with her life. She started going out at times. This was different for her children because we were used to her being at home. We found out later that our parent was divorced. She started going out with this guy name Sonny Man. It was pretty hard seeing this man with our mother but we had to accept who she was with. We knew in our hearts that she was hurt and lonely. Over time we tried to accept him. He was turning out to be a nice guy.

One day he asked my mother to marry him, I guess my mother thought about it for a little while and eventually said yes and they got married. My mother had 6 kids and needed some help. We thought maybe things would get back to normal. Well it didn't get back to normal; my stepfather wanted my mother to go out with him every weekend. Sometimes she would go and sometimes she didn't. When she stayed home he would say you think more of your children than you do me. It wasn't long until he would start threatening my mother if she didn't do whatever he said. Now when Sonny man was not drinking he was a nice person.

It was when he was drinking it got scary. One Saturday, my brother and I were standing in the kitchen in front of the refrigerator talking. My stepfather stood outside at the kitchen window watching us. He pulled out a pistol and shot the gun between us hitting the refrigerator with a loud boom. We knew then that this man didn't care if he'd killed one of us.

The police arrested him that day, but he didn't stay in jail that long. He was right back at the house apologizing and ask to come back. Later my mother took him back if he promised to quit drinking. He did quit for a few months and then started back. It was tough times for the family. He started threaten my mom life when he was drinking. He had to leave town because he was too much trouble or stay in jail. He chose to leave town and move to this smaller town called "Homerville Ga." He talked my mother into moving with him with all her children.

We thought this was the worse decision that she could ever make but she was afraid of him and went alone with anything he said. My brother refused to move with us. He thought he wanted to kill him because he looked a lot like my dad, so he moved to Daytona Beach with my Aunt Lois. Now there was nothing in Homerville but pine trees and turpentine. He worked on a plantation dipping turpentine. It would be maybe 10 to 15 black men in the woods dipping turpentine from the pine trees. The owner would have his sons riding though the wood on horses checking on the men. One of the sons would come and pick me up from home and ride me on the back of his horse. We would ride through the woods checking on the men. As a child, it was painful seeing all these black men in the woods like slaves walking through the woods dipping turpentine. Well you know a few weeks later my stepfather got drunk and began chasing my mother with a pistol. I told my mom to run. We took off running up the highway and anytime a car would pass we would lay down in the grass to keep from being seen. While we were running it gave my sisters time to go get help. So the owner of the plantation and the police were searching for us as well. We ran for a couple hours. The police finally caught up with us and later caught Sonny Man. He was held until he was sober, and then was told that he would have to leave. Again, we had to pack and leave town. Sonny Man sobered up for a few weeks and had contact one of his sisters in New York and had arrange for the family to move up there. The plans were that we would work on the farm. My mother still had her old 55 Buick so we packed up all we could take and headed to New York, passing through Waycross. My sister Brenda was scared to death of Sonny Man and didn't want to go with him, so we wind up leaving her with a friend with the intentions of picking her up later. The remaining girls and myself went to New York with my mother. We drove my mom's 55 Buick and again when we went over 50 it rock side to side. When we got up near D.C., the kids were sleep in the back seat and was awakened by a bear jumping the bridge after we had hit him with the Buick. We couldn't go back to sleep after that, we looked for more Bears for the rest of the night. No more Bears, we made it to New York safe. Things was great for the first few months. It was apple trees all around us and my mom loved making apple pies. Now my family stayed up in the loft (the attic) it was different but okay. All around us was beautiful mountains (Whaling New York). Just across the street right in front of the house you could look down and see the town about a mile or two down the mountain below in the valley.

We were enrolled in school, and the students were Black and Puerco Rican. I met this little Rican girl and she was nice to me and very pretty. The only problem was the Rican boys didn't like that. This little short boy came to me with his knife out telling me to stay away from her. School was still great. (Now this was a nice change even with the threats from the Rican boys.) I should have noticed when things started to change.

One day my stepfather Sonny Man was driving the Buick and when he got out of the car he left it out of gear. The car started rolling backward toward the cliff. I jumped in the car screaming the car is going down the cliff. I turn the steering wheel guiding the car into the ditch stopping it from going off the cliff. I was a hero for a while but that day we realized he had started drinking again. He started demanding again that my mother go out with him, and again she did.

I had never seen my mom drink, she would love sitting around telling us stories of her childhood and how she used to love climbing. Now we were up in New York my mom and 4 of her children. I think one reason why my mom didn't mind coming to New York was that my dad was in New Jersey. It didn't matter he may as well have been a thousand miles away. We never saw him.

Brenda was still in Georgia and Andrew was in Daytona Beach with my Aunt. Sleeping in the loft began to get crazy, at night you could hear everything that was said. My stepfather use to tell my mother she would "look pretty in her grave." He would tell her in a pink dress. It was this and many other things he would say to her that frighten us. Sometime I would be in bed nervous and tensed up fearing the worse. Him telling her one day he would kill her and sometime all her children. So, you know we feared him and all I could think about was how I could kill him before he killed or hurt one of us. I feared every day that he might kill my mom. It is a helpless feeling when your family life is in danger and there's nothing that you can do about it. One Friday my mother took all the kids down town in the valley shopping. She saw this cross-eyed lady and made a joke about her eyes. I didn't think it was funny and felt bad for the lady. That night my stepfather made my mom go out with him. She didn't want to but she went anyway, my mom was a pretty little shorty and I guess he like showing her off. She had long natural black curly hair and light tan completion.

She told us that she would be back in a little while. They must have left around 9:00 p.m. Between 11:30 pm and 12:00 a.m., they still had not come back and we began to get worried. 1:00 a.m. came they still weren't back. 2:00 a.m. to 2:30 a.m., still no mom. This wasn't like mom. Between 3:30 and 4:00 a.m., we heard this car roaring by speeding up and down the mountain. This car must have done this for at least an hour. I guess around 5:00am we heard this car speeding by and a loud boom and the car flipping several times maybe 5 or 6 time and then total silent. I remember all of us awake and crying saying please God don't let that be my mama. We wait and waited and continued praying and hoping that was not our mom. I remembered every time the car was speeding by that night, I would hold the side of the bed in a death grip.

Now just at daylight there coming in the kitchen door my stepfather cursing this lady that I knew was not my mom. Her head was twice the size of my mom and she had very big lips and eyes. And she was much darker with dried blood in her hair and running down her face. My sisters and I stood there in shock as we realized that this was our mother. My mother had blue and black bruises all up and down her body (she was normally a light pecan tan). I remember crying out loud and saying that's not my mama over and over again. Mean time this man was still cursing my mom out.

I also found out later that he had beaten my mother after the accident that morning. I felt so helpless that I couldn't kill him on the spot. I was about 8 to 9 years of age at this time and I knew I had to do something fast. Later me and my sisters went to see where they had crashed and the car was turned upside down in the ditch. The ditch was the only thing that stopped the car from going over the cliff. My mother was never taken to a hospital. Another day came and things didn't get better. I prayed to God everyday asking him to kill this man or take him out of our life. I think this man taught me to hate, because all I could think of is seeing him dead, sometimes feeling guilty because I didn't kill him.

A few weeks went by and my mother was healing and beginning to look like herself again. My stepfather was still drinking and threatening my mom and the rest of us. One Friday he drew a pistol on my mom again and my sisters were standing their screaming along with my mom. I told my mom to run and the girls would follow her so that's what she did. We started to run and did not look back. We ran about 2 miles up the road and hiding in the woods when a car passed by. There were about 4 or 5 teenage children at the house and they hide us there until the next morning. Their parents were away for a few days. My stepfather came by their house and they told him we weren't there. The next morning early, we knew we had to leave and go to try to find help. It was a migration work camp about another mile up the road and we walked there for help. My step father came there several times looking for us but they hide us in one of the rooms. The last time he came he got in a fight with the workers, drawing his knife on the workers. He winds up getting into a knife fight and got a knife broken off into his arm. The New York police took him away and told him to never come back into the state of New York.

Now my family had nowhere to go so the contractor of the migrant worker allowed us to stay in the camp and work in the fields with the rest of the workers. Again, we left everything behind and left with just the clothes on our backs. My oldest sister and I worked in the fields picking potatoes. As time passed, my mom started talking this man named Eugene. At the end of the season, we went back south to Florida

With the rest of the workers to work in the cabbages patches. They said my sister and I were to young so they wouldn't let us work. We stayed in Spuds, Florida and went back up the road the next year to Saint James, Long Island, New York. My sister, Mease, was 13 or 14 and got in an argument with Eugene. She left home, going to stay with the Callaway crew and we went with another crew.

When school was back in I was going to the fourth grade but I couldn't go to school because I had to work. I remember seeing the school bus pass by every day while I was in the fields. My 2 younger sisters were allowed to go to school but I wasn't. We worked and save up enough money to get another car. My mom and boyfriend Eugene went out and bought a car. We had the car less than a week and Eugene crash it totaling it on the side of a mountain and didn't get a scratch on him. Every penny that I made was saved for that new car. But her boyfriend was another drinker and began to become abusive. When the season was over in New York the bus that we rode up on was broken down so we had to ride on the back of a "Flat Bed Truck" all the way from up State New York to Florida. (About 25 people on the back). That was far most the scariest trip I have ever made in my life and the longest one. We made it back to Florida but this time moved to Hasting Florida, in Mr. Charlie Morman's Quarters. This was a black gentleman and had a little store in his quarters. We were supposed to be riding back in a new car. Now when we moved to Hasting, my mom enrolled us into school. By this time, I was in the 5th grade. Now the Christmas before my oldest sister was still with us and we had 3 candy bars a piece and that was our Christmas. This coming Christmas I looking for about the same. Well Christmas Day to my surprise

I got a big "Red Wing" bicycle, and a box full of all kind of other toys. And my sisters had a great Christmas as well. Now I found out later that my mom friend didn't like her spending money on us like that. Something happened and I don't know exactly what, but she wanted to leave Hasting as soon as possible, leaving everything behind again. One Monday morning, school time, Mr. Charlie Morman and my mom told me to ride my bicycle up 208 to I-95 and keep riding and talk to no one. They picked me up about 5 miles south on I-95 he picked me and my back up and took us to Daytona Beach. Thank God for Mr. Morman. He took us to my Aunt Lois house in Pine Haven. His sister owned Nick's package store just down the street from my aunt. All this time my Aunt was just 50 miles away. Maybe my mother knew this but didn't want to come because this was my dad's sister, but we were here now and I was happy.

Note: *For days, my aunt would wash my mother's hair and every time she did so, you could see the blood washed from her scalp. My mother told me "Tony they tried to kill me." But still she was alive. She was alive.*

CHAPTER 4

We arrived in Daytona Beach and Mr. Morman knew exactly where 755 Pine Haven was. It was a huge apartment complex that was a city block long and a city block wide. It had beautiful pine trees all over the complex, everywhere. It had beautiful grass, and the scenery. I guess my mother had called my Aunt Lois and she was expecting us. Now my aunt had 4 children of her own and my brother Andrew. Now my mother and 3 more children were added to the house hold. For a few months, maybe about 9 sometimes, 10 people lived in a 3-bed room apartment.

I had a girl cousin name Barbara that was the same age as me, and Greg and Tara younger siblings. I wanted to surprise my cousins by walking toward the school by the route they walk home. As I walked near the school I seen and heard this big crowd of children walking and talking about this big fight that was about to happen. They were saying that she was going to tear that boy up. As I got closer I found out that they were talking about my "first cousin Barbara". That day I found out that she didn't play.

We stayed with my aunt for a few months, and I was enrolled in Banner Elementary. My first day of school, my mother was working. My aunt boyfriend, Big Boy, had gotten my mother a job working at a seafood restaurant called Anchor Inn. I enrolled myself. Because I didn't have school records and my mother didn't want anyone to know where we were there was never records. They put me back in fifth with my younger sister. They said I didn't look big enough to be in 6th grade. I wanted to be in my right grade but I know that I was out of school for a while I was okay. A few months down the road my mother found a new project complex called "Caroline Village" that was just build and we were one of the first families that moved in. It was a big complex with dirt road. They hadn't been paved yet. It was right in front of Campbell Junior and Senior High, life was getting better and better. Turie T. Small elementary, two blocks from the house.

In 1966 I was the paperboy for News Journal and I threw papers in South Street. The kids in the neighborhood would always try to steal my bicycle, and the money that was in the bag for News Papers. I would keep it in my sight at all times. South Street was a tough route so that job didn't last long.

No one wanted to pay their bill but they were always complaining. It was like working for nothing. Rather than dealing with them, I started throwing the newspapers in the ditch. My brother, on the other hand, went to the Air Force right out of high school and that was a proud moment for the family. One thing that I learned about my brother and first cousin was that they had a lot of women and they called them by our home town name, i.e. "Waycross".

Lil Cross, Big Cross, and me, they named "Tony Waycross". Every time I saw my brother, he was happy and he would always have a different girl over to the house. When those girls would see me out they would say, "you are Cross' little brother". When he was at home, he would clean up by moving all the furniture, dusting, sweeping, mopping and waxing the whole house. Not like me... I clean around stuff. My brother would always sing songs like (Rainbow 65) "I want to ask you one thing a baby---I want to ask you one thing baby, I want to ask you one thing," and if he wasn't singing that song he was saying the poem, "I THINK I SHOULD NEVER SEE A POEM AS BEAUTIFUL AS A TREE". So, it seemed that all the males in my family was Waycross. I had a cousin from Brooklyn New York, that had a bad drug problem (my dad side of the family) my mom let him stay with us for a little while he slept in my room in Caroline Village. He would bring drugs into the room and tell me if I say anything he would kill me. I kept my mouth shut. My mother came in the room one time and ask where this big plant come from. It was a Marijuana Plant. I didn't tell my mom what it was. Pete hung out with Don and Na and they would always be working on something. Mostly an old car they used to drive around. This was in the Mid 60s and they all had on their due rags. My cousin Pete talked like he had a frog in his throat, but with a New York accent. I was still a paper boy and my paper money began to become missing and I would ask Pete about it, he would say I haven't seen no damn money. Don't ask me about it no more. Boy was I glad when he finally moved.

He was not always like that, as kids he was at least 10 or more years older than me and use to play football in high school. He would always bring his team mates over to his house for brownies that his grandmother would make for them my great aunt Fannie. Every now and then he would let me hang out. He was a very different person.

By the time I got to high school I was well known because of my brother and cousins. I was growing up and had my group of friends. I was still getting into trouble but not getting caught most of the time. That same year we found out that Brenda my sister that stayed back in Waycross was still there. My first cousin, Bro Shake, his girlfriend and my brother went back to Waycross and picked her up from school and brought her back. By the end of the year she was back with the rest of the family. Now my oldest sister Mease was still going back and forth up the road she was about 17 by now and was the camp cook and had a little girl. In 1967 my brother had a little girl. My mother was a grandmother. In about May of 1968 was the first time I saw my father sense they had divorced. He brought with him a little girl name Sherri that was my little sister about 2 years old, very beautiful little girl. He never sent my mother anything to help us but he brought all the kids a present when he came. He brought me a "Green Shark Skin Suit" I put it in the cleaners and someone broke in and stole it. I never had a chance to wear it. We had a great time even my mother for a little while things seem like old times again. My parent laughing and talking it was great. My father never did anything else for his kids but we never stopped loving him. Now I remember the times when black police officers couldn't arrest white people at all they had to call a white officer to make the arrest, but white policeman could arrest black people. I remember I went to the Fair on City Island with 2 of my buddies and on the way back 2 White men was standing by their car talking. The smallest kid (Rambo) pick up a hand full of rocks and threw them and hit the man car. Me and Wallace the other kid looked at him in anger and couldn't do nothing but run. We were at least 2 miles from home. The police started chasing us and me and Rambo was about a ½ mile from home behind the school in a big open field.

Wallace went another route and we didn't see him. It was a big ditch that ran across the school and I jumped in it and told Rambo to jump in it too. He stood there in the open saying he was tired and was giving up. The police pulled up to him and I continued hiding. They ask him where was his friends after a couple times asking, Rambo said come on out Tony they know you are down there. I didn't say nothing and he called me a second time and the policeman join in saying come on out. I climbed out of the ditch angry at Rambo because he was the one that started this and then told on me. It was in the middle of shift change for the policeman and they normally turn you over to black policeman if you are black. While we were in the back seat of the car the policeman was talking about the black policeman in an insulting way. When they turned us over to the black policeman the first thing they did was criticized another black policeman. We couldn't help but laugh. They took us home and told my mother what had happened. I was in trouble; she was sleep and had to go to work to her second job. I had no intention of getting into trouble that night so I was careful who hung out with and knew when it was time to leave from then on. We were healthy, alive and we were doing O.K. by ourselves. My mom was working 2 jobs, and I worked in the restaurant after school. My brother sent money home to help with the bills. I always went out for football and made first string but my mom would always come or send my sisters to get me off the field to go to work. She would say work and help out your family or we can go on welfare and get help. We never went on welfare.

 A couple months later in summer of 1968 we got more company. I walked in the house and a very bright skinned lady and old white lady was sitting in our living room. I went to my mom and asked her who was that old white lady in our living room. She told me it was my Aunt Veal. and my mother's Grandma Agnes, whom I had never met. I found that I had a huge and beautiful family that I didn't know anything about. I only knew of my mom's oldest sister in Lumber City, Georgia. I had a great uncle in Miami that was a police officer. Relatives started showing up from everywhere.

Note: *During some of those times my aunt Veal and my grandmother visited, they brought my 1st cousin Gwen with them; she was around the age of my brother Andrew. Myself and Aunt Veal and Uncle Ed's three boys would try and play touchy - touchy with Gwen and wind up touching Grandma by mistake. (You see the lights were off) just being boys.*

Now my Grandpa Charlie started visiting us and I don't know if my mom planned it or not but my Grandmother coincidently was visiting the same time as my grandfather. My grandparents had been divorced for over 51 years and hadn't seen or heard from each other since then. Man, they hit it off the first day and they never departed after that. My grandmother moved from Chattanooga, Tennessee to Scotland, Ga. To live with my granddad and they both died in the same house. My grandfather died first and my grandmother died 3 years later. She didn't want to live without him. They were really happy together. I met so many relatives that I didn't know I had and we started talking about family reunions. They were developing a new subdivision up the street from the projects, between Campbell High and Turie T. Small Elementary and my mother wanted to buy us a home. She had a friend, an older man, that was dating her, and he helped make it happen alone with her children. We moved into our new home on Russell Dr. in 1968... our first new home. This was before integration and Campbell was 7th thru 12th grade. I could jump the ditch and be at school every day.

My mother bought a 1965 brand new Galaxy 500 powder blue. When she went to sleep, I would take the car out of gear and roll it out of the driveway and have it back home before she got up. I got away with it for a good while. One night I had a date and called myself driving behind the Cypress Street pool and got the car stuck in drive. It would not go into reverse. When I finally got the car back home I couldn't pull in the driveway I knew it wouldn't go into reverse. Needless to say, she was hot. I didn't stop borrowing the car but I was very careful from then on. My friend Jeff did the same thing with his mother's car; she had a 65 Chevy Impala "blue and white. We would be all over the place in that car.

I remember one day we rode the car in the woods and Jeff had me and 2 other buddies in the car. We were deep in the woods and Jeff put the car in reverse and speeded in reverse all the way through the woods. When we got out of the woods all 4 of the tires were flat. The police were on the corner and saw us. We were already shaking up from the ride and now I knew we were going to jail. Instead the policeman offered to help. He gave us a ride to Johnson Gas Station and Mr. Johnson repaired all the tires. We had dodged another bullet.

At the age of 18 during this time the legal age. You were considered legal because of the "Viet Nam area". We weren't quite 18 but could always get a buddy to buy whatever we wanted for a beer. This was the thing that guys our age loved to do, sneaking to the clubs and hanging out at the "Bottom" (Black Clubs). Every now and then we were threatened by guys we didn't get alone with and had guns drawn on us. A guy drew a shot gun on me about a girl that I dated in 10th grade and told me that I was to stay away from her. I hadn't talked this girl for a while but he felt threatened. We didn't have sense enough to be scared or to stop what we were doing. We thought it made us bad dudes when other guys felt threatened by our mere presence. Too funny.

One day Jeff had borrowed his mom's car again and had his nephew, in his underwear, riding with him. His mom was in church and came out just in time to see Jeff in her car. She made him get out of the car in the middle of the streets and snatched the baby out, too. When he finally got home, he got his butt kicked. Jeff had an older brother, Buddy, who always kept me and Jeff in check. His other brother Vern always laughed at us because he knew we deserved it. Vern never got into trouble, unlike Jeff and me. I became best of friends with their family, and went to their family reunions quite often. When Jeff would call himself running away from home, he would come to my house and his mother would call mine, and say, "Don't tell him I called." and would leave him there. Later he would go back home and take his punishment like a man.

I reflect on this time before integration, the race riots, when John F. Kennedy, Dr. Martin Luther King, Jr. and even the murder of Malcolm X. I was a young boy but I remember watching buildings burn down. When Dr. King died, there were a lot of upset black people. They were burning down everything in sight. I was watching a store burn down when this man came from behind, put a pistol to my head, and said, "If you say another word I will kill you". The older guys talked him down. The guy worked at the store that they were burning down and was watching his job go up in flames.

I met some of Malcolm X's soldiers running from the Nation of Islam. Me and a couple other friends would hang out at their place smoke a little weed and listen to some of the stories they would tell us. This was during the Vietnam war and a lot was going on.

1969 was the first year of integration, and Campbell was no longer a high school. The Blacks had to be bused to Mainland High School. The first year, there were a lot of fights. There were so many students that they had to have a split session, morning and noon. It seemed that it was the Black people who had to adjust and give up everything. We were the ones being bused, losing friends and being separated from family members. We did not have the same teachers or administrators and Black principals became a thing of the past. All the students had a hard time coping. This was the first time in American history that Southern Blacks and Whites went to school together, and no one seemed happy about it.

I guess every city had their Apollo Time in their town. Well, ours was held every year at Bethune Cookman College gym. It was mostly Black groups and single talent from mostly Black schools.

Well, me and my buddy Jeff were recruited in 8th and 9th grade, off the football team to perform in what we call the "Jabba Walt" (Jabberwock). Campbell Junior High won the award 2 years in a row. (Me and this girl name Dorothy had the leading parts both year). By the time we got to Mainland we were known by Mrs. Bettye Bethune (a black P.E. coach at Mainland). Mrs. Bethune decided to enter Mainland in the Jabberwock, and her theme was the movie, "Hang 'Em High," so we were all dressed like cowboys and did a little Western skit. The reason a lot of guys agreed to it was that we knew a lot of pretty and fine girls would be there. We had a lot of football players volunteering. Now this new guy on campus asked me about a certain girl in the play that he had an interest in. I told him to come and join the play and he would meet a lot of pretty girls like that. He responded to me saying no, the "Drama Class" is where the money is. This was in our 11th grade year. You can find his picture in the 1971 year book, Mainland Sr. High his name was "Denzel Washington". This was brought to my attention years after he became famous.

Now all through most of Junior High and Senior High I was into smoking pot and other drugs. The 60s and 70s were the years of the "Flower Child or Children" Hippies. Blacks and Whites found things they could do together. I had my White, Black, and Native American friends that I used to play hooky and get high with. Needless to say, the Administration got wind of it and stated searching all suspects on campus. Some was obvious since they were passing out in class. I was fortunate that I didn't get in trouble.

I had this game plan that the first part of the school year every year I would dress tacky. Then I would wear a different outfit every da., I would at times wear a nice tie and the bell bottom pants and big buckle belt. Keep my "Afro" in tack. I would get a lot of compliments on my outfits, from teachers and students. I would go shopping as far as Tampa or Jacksonville to buy my clothes and just hang them in the closet until what I felt was the opportune moment. Usually that was after everyone else had worn their new "school clothes". I had girlfriends off and on but never committed myself. This one girl caught my attention in my Science class so I would always act a fool to get her attention. We had a pretty cool science teacher and he would not get offended for small disruptions. I would take a stool, sit it on the lab table and sit on the stool for her attention. It got her attention and we dated all through high school. That did not stop me from pushing the envelope though and I still got in my share of trouble, and made a lot of bad decisions.

I remember one night while my mom was at work. Around the age of 16 to 17, me and one of my buddies called Stinker went over to another buddy's house to hang out and get high. We called him Jo. His mother and sisters had left town and Jo had the house to himself. His stepfather was abusive and was in prison. So, we came over often, it was our party house or so we thought. This night we had the music turned up loud and the house filled with smoke. There were about 5 or 6 of us. We normally had 2 or 3 girls over but this night there were about 5 guys and scattered all through the house. The house was an old wooden house with squeaky floors, that made that squeaky sound every time you walked. The porch was even worse. The old porch had a lot of junk on it. Around about 10 o'clock that night out of nowhere came a big thump on the porch. Nobody wanted to go and see what it was. Most of us speculated that it was Jo's step dad coming home and that he had broken out of prison. Nobody dared go to the door. All 5 of us went into this one bedroom and sat in one place, not moving and we did very little talking. One of the guys was so afraid that he laid in the bed, in the fetal position all night trembling and moaning out loud. All of us sat in the same position until the sun came up the next morning. It appeared that someone or something was trying to break into the house. After that we decided to give the party house a break for a while.

Moving right along...still getting into more trouble hanging out with this buddy I had from Tampa named TJ. He came to visit and brought two other friends with him. They drove this old 55 Rambler (nice little ride) and would go around to the clothing stores (boosting) shop lifting. I was in class, learning to be a thief. You went in the store and took about 5 or 6 pairs of pants in the fitting room, put about 4 on and put your regular pants on top of them and walked out of the store. Those crazy guys had me up and down the road with them. TJ stayed on 22nd in the Projects and there were several clubs and Pools halls right across the street from his house. He was well known in the area for some of the things he was into. He was also the type of guy that believed in payback. I remember him getting jumped by 4 or 5 boys, and one by one he caught up with them and beat them down. TJ fought dirty and for keeps. He would pick up anything he could find and sneak up behind you. You know the rest. A lot of older guys in Tampa were afraid of him.

We hung out for a while going back and forth to Tampa until one day TJ and one of his friends from Tampa came by my house. His buddy had some weed and wanted me and my next-door neighbor to try it. I was O.K. with that but he wanted to hold the "Joint" and give me a "Shot Gun" (That's blowing the smoke up each nostril.) after the second time, with him trying to blow it in my face, I slapped his hand, knocking the lit joint in his face. Then he tried to flick the joint in my face so you know it was a standoff. Now we were at a standoff. TJ's position was that he had to take sides with his home boy from Tampa because he had to go back home. That ended our friendship.

But there was still enough trouble right here at home for me to get into.

Let's just say that someone had a car and he let one of his friends borrow it. They came back twice with case after case of alcohol, so much that it almost filled one room. For a long time, we didn't have to worry about alcohol. I had buddies that turned me on to "Sunshine (LSD). One day we went over to one of his buddy's house on our 10 speed bikes. He was a white life guard and we sat around smoking for a while. He then pulls out a small tab and served it on ice cream. When I tell you that we were two blocks from our neighborhood and couldn't find our way home I am not exaggerating. A black guy let us hold on to the back of his car until we got to the projects. After that night, we did what we called psychedelic drugs quite often.

This was just to name a couple of things that could have sent me away for a long time. A lot of these guys are no longer living. Some are doing time in prison and I know a few that went crazy. I had one friend that started out losing his fingers and toes a little at a time and then both legs. He continued to use and eventually died. You can be "foolish only for so long before it catches up with you. Unfortunately, these are not the worse drugs that were introduced into the black community and we are paying a stiff price because of foolish decisions.

Now my brother on the other hand was in Thailand for two years then the Philippines for about two years. In 1971 he got out the military and he stayed at home for a while. He would never go in the room and sleep, he would take a bath and put all his clothes back on and sleep in the living room. One day I shook him to tell him to go and get in the bed and he jump up and said if you ever put your hands on me I will kill you. From that moment on I felt that I had lost my brother, he was never again the person he was before his experiences in the military.

I loved him but we started having problems because we kept getting our bags of weed mixed up. We were always arguing about who's bag it was. Yes, we still shared a room...well, we had a little Sausage dog named Marco and in the bed room we had a water bed. The dog loved to come in and lay on the water bed. One day we got home and we're looking for our pot. Marco was lying on the bed and wouldn't move. I looked in the corner and saw he had eaten a whole bag of "Pot"... Columbia Gold...the best! Boy, I got angry and so did my brother. I took him to the front door to kick him out; he was so high he fell out the front door passed out. We couldn't help but burst out laughing.

My cousin and some of his buddies became one of the biggest suppliers in the area. They would always ride around in 2 or 3 cars and their woman with them. They would keep a couple apartments or have women rent them and they would stay there. When my brother came home he would hang out with them.

I remember one time my brother came home on leave and wanted to borrow my car. (Backing up a little) I was in the 11th grade and had a 1965 Chevy Impala, Metallic Blue. I told them if I went with them he could use my car. He agreed to it. I was driving to what we called the Bottom. His conditions were that I smoke some of the joint they were smoking and yes, I agreed. After hitting it a couple times I was high. The car was full guys and girls and they were laughing at me and I didn't know why. My brother finally told me to speed up and I said I put the gas pedal to the floor. I looked at the "Speed Odometer" I was going 5 miles an hour. Well, they took me home and I didn't see my car for the next 2 to 3 days.

Again, when my brother got out of the service and for a while he and my cousin began doing barbs and uppers and a lot of other things. One day he almost over dosed and my aunt took him to the hospital to be pumped out. About two weeks after that my brother had been in the room sleeping steadily for about three days and I couldn't hide him anymore nor could I wake him up. We took him to the hosp. and he had to be pumped out AGAIN.

My mother used to find drugs in our room and hide them in the glove compartment of her car hiding them from us. We used to call her "Shorty the Bust Lady". My cousin got so into this drug thing that when my mom was at work at night they would come to our house to test the drugs. They would get a junkie to shoot the drugs and test them. They would have grocery bags full. After a while my brother moved away to Lakeland and got a job. Mean time I still had a job at Anchor Inn and worked until I graduated.

Now I had another cousin that was on my mother's side and he talked me into going down to

Miami, so I quit my job. Before we left for Miami we were down at the Bottom and someone hollowed "Freeze". That was the nick name of the guy who was partners with my cousin and we thought someone was calling him. But after the gun shots we knew it was time to move on.

This was my chance to get out of Daytona. It was too slow and I was ready to go and for the first time be on my own. I felt like a bird that had been imprisoned in a cage and had been set free. I know that I had enemies even the more, because I was hanging out with what the local guys considered the Miami boys. They knew they were different by the way they dressed, always ahead of Daytona. They considered Daytona slow. They would say it's like being in the country. I couldn't see myself advancing here in Daytona and was glad to move on. I kind of left everything even my girlfriend behind. All I could think of at the time was Miami Beach, Florida.

We were headed down 95 south. I had been to Miami several times when I was younger and fell in love with it. I had nothing particular in mind as far as how I would live, but I didn't care. My fast-talking cousin would say don't worry about it, don't worry about. So, I didn't worry about it. We rode and got high, having a great time all the way down.

Chapter 5

Now Jack had an old International Heinemann car, a little box car. We drove from Daytona to about 20 miles from Miami and blew the engine by not putting oil into the car, we were still happy just to get in Miami.

Freeze was from Carol City and had someone to pick us up. We towed the car to Freeze's house and left it there. Me and Ike went on to Liberty City and got a room on 63rd and 17th over the pool hall. It was in the middle of the summer and the rooms didn't have A.C... So, that night we went to Browns Bar & Night Club, Betty Wright performed at this Club and used to stay in the area. This club had mirrors that covered the walls all the way around the club. Me, my cousin and several other people were standing outside the club when a yellow Mercury pulled up right in front of us (in front of the club). They pulled out a rifle and started shooting at the guy next to me. As we ran, the guy stayed right beside me. I remember thinking I wish he would run somewhere else. This was an exciting night a "drive by" on the first night in Miami.

When we got back to the room it was so hot that we slept with the door open. Around about 4 a.m., my cousin woke up and said "man, why are you rubbing my leg", and I replied "you must be crazy". At that time, the 2 gay guys that had a room next door to us was sneaking out the room laughing like little girls. From then on, we closed the door and took the heat, no matter how hot it got.

We were about out of money and needed some income fast so we went looking for a job in Hialeah. There were a lot of warehouses out this way. We both found jobs at Winn Dixie warehouse. We must have worked about 2 weeks and realized it was hard work and both decided not to go back. We had an Uncle name Kelly that had a Gas station on 14th street in "Over Town" between Liberty City and Down Town Miami. I talked him into giving me a job but Ike had other plans.

I worked at the station and my uncle sold the Numbers they called Cuba. You could play for as low as 50 cents and make $60.00 if you hit. I did hit a couple times. I would borrow money from the drawer every now and then to play. My uncle was very out spoken and sometimes he scared me the way he would curse out some of his costumers. I would say Uncle Kelly calm down and he would say out loud f_ _ _ k him or them. We had kids that came by the station to buy brakes fluid all the time and I asked why. These kids would always keep a wash cloth or a rag with them. I found out that they were getting high off the brake fluid. It was a big thing in Miami among the young kids. I would say "if you know that they are getting high off it, why do you sell it to them". He would say "hell if they don't buy it from me they'll go somewhere else and buy it". Well now I knew why we keep so much brake fluid in stock now.

    It was fun working at the station but I knew I had to eventually move on. Jack had been back and forth with other plans and decided to try them out and I quit working with my uncle. We used the money to do other things. The next night we went to this club called the Paradise (The Pool) I think what it meant was the pool of women. It was a city block long and a city block wide. It was the biggest club I had ever seen. And it had some of the most beautiful women you ever wanted to see.

    Around the club, you would see what we called Fly Guys just watching. I found out quick that those guys were "Pimps and those beautiful women were their women (their stable). Those guys were driving new Cadillacs, Mercedes Benz, Continentals all kinds of big cars. You would see the Pimps pull up in their cars and their women following them in other nice cars. Some rode their women with them. One pimp with the street name "James Brown" owned his own Trans house that was right in front of the club and had about 12 women working for him. A Pimp with street name "Do Nasty" had about 10 women and had them driving behind him in 2 Mark 4 Continentals. He was from Ft. Lauderdale (They said they called him "Do Nasty "because he made his women do anything to make money). There was one pimp who called himself "Jerry Butler" and he had 3 women that rode with him. Sometimes they drove another car. Jerry used to brag about how his main woman Peaches made mega money, sometimes 5 or 6 grand a night. At times robbing her tricks.

The club (The Pool) had Trans (Whore houses) houses on each side of the club with older ladies sitting at a table under an umbrella collecting money for renting rooms, corner to corner on both sides of the club. I had never seen nothing like it.

The women would not stay in one place and they would continually walk from one end of the club to the other side asking if you want a date. I had gotten relaxed and knew almost everybody.

My cousin was down there because he wanted to learn the game. His attitude was that since he caught his girlfriend cheating on him and since she like doing it so much, they might as well make money. He had a couple of women and he went into the game and it wasn't long before we had enough money to buy a car and move to downtown Miami. His problem was he would try me every now and then. He would try and tell me what to do like I was his "Do Boy", and I wasn't having it. I wasn't a pimp but I considered myself a hustler and I demanded respect like he wanted respect. I know he was my older cousin. That's just the way you had to be in the streets.

A pimp is like a wolf praying on helpless sheep, these guys would steal each other women; they would go to small country towns and charm these country girls with their nice cars and diamond rings. They would make them promises and a lot of them would go for it, and when they realized what they are doing they are trapped and at the mercy of the pimp. A lot of them were brought from other states and a long way from home. Let the Pimp Tales continue… Now there was this "Fag name Turkey" that wore long Maxi dresses and kept a 357 Magnum between his legs. He would always sell out to me and point at his pistol. This guy made his money by being a hooker and made more money than the average woman. A lot of times he robbed his tricks. We moved to The Taj Apartments. We stayed on the fifth floor and found out Jerry Butler stayed on the seventh floor. This was a seventeen-story building with a penthouse and pool on the roof. We would sleep until about 3or 4 o'clock and go swimming in the evenings. And late at night we would be out until the sun was almost up.

We were living the life and making money selling other products. Living at the Taj, I met Clarence Reid (Blow Fly). He stayed on the 7th floor, and was working out of a recording studio on Miami Beach. I would see him some mornings going to work. He had this young girl staying with him from Tennessee that would hang out with us while he was at work. Most the time we would be at the penthouse on the roof.

Now "Blow Fly" was a dirty rapper. There was this mixed couple, Nick and Lisa that stayed on the fifth floor and Lisa loved hanging out at the apartment. Lisa was black and had a little Chihuahua that looked just like her. Nick didn't like her hanging around us so much and had this conversation with me about him being in the mob, sort of warning me who he was. He really didn't have anything to worry about she was made just for him.

Jerry Butler started to call me "Young Blood". Now a Pimp's game is that if he can make another so called pimp respect him enough that he can make him his "Do boy". Jerry knew that a few women liked me and would try to compliment me and cut down my cousin. Kind of a way to try and turn me against him. You see Jerry wanted Jack's so called stable and tried anything he could think of even to disrespect Jack, things like asking Jack to pick him up a newspaper. This way the other guy would show control over him as being weak. Then he would try to steal his women saying he is too weak to be a "Pimp". If a woman wanted to choose you to be their pimp, they would come up to you and ask you to be their daddy.

I was out their hustling but I didn't care much about the Pimp Game. I thought about my 5 sisters and mother and other females. I used to tell my cousin that it takes a weak man to have a woman on the streets selling their body. Now the Hustling we used to do somethings on credit and some would not pay up. So, we had to get some respect so we talked about a drive by. We rode up on the guy and had a little 25 automatic. He was at an outdoor restaurant and no one wanted to do anything. We chickened out, thank God. A Pimp's game was that a lot of them read and know the Bible and win women over by quoting "the Word". Saying things like God helps them that help themselves. That's not even in the Bible.

I had a running partner named Jimmie. He was a black Puerto Rican who was darker than me and he spoke Spanish better than English but spoke both well. He would be great for getting deals with Cubans and other Spanish speaking people. He hooked me up with the Spanish Tailors and I had suits made and shoes. They could make anything. I was still staying with Jack but we were growing apart, arguing all the time and never agreeing. (Almost everyone used the Bible to play the game.) Jimmie had a Spanish Bible he used to walk around with. We were going to this Club one night called Soul Place and two detectives offered us a ride to the club and we accepted. The same guys earlier the week before were in Downtown Miami and asked me to follow them into a couple of clothing stores pointing out clothes for me to steal for them. I told them that I don't steal. So, they wanted to catch us doing anything they could.

Me and Jimmie were sitting in back seat and they had a briefcase in the backseat and we asked them what's in the briefcase. We let them know that we knew they was Cops and to quit playing games. And they told us if we spit on the ground we were going to prison. Now we changed locations for a while hanging out in "Coconut Grove" it was like being in the country. I left Miami shortly after that.

The plan was that I went back to Daytona for a while and my partner Jimmie went to Brooklyn to set things up for me to follow him up. But things didn't work out in Brooklyn. Jimmie wound up robbing some guy and came back to Daytona. I knew that I couldn't have him around my people long. My mother worked at night and liked Jimmie. Both my mother and sisters thought he was so polite. My best friend in high school came down to visit from Atlanta and that was my way out of Daytona.

I decided to move to Atlanta. I told Jimmie he had to move on and I moved to Atlanta with my friend Jeff. I had winter clothes that Jimmie brought back from Brooklyn. We were always making deals with each other. I hated leaving Jimmie like that but when you are used to going you don't let nothing hold you up. I left this guy in my home town not knowing what he was really capable of doing. Thank God for his grace and mercy.

That year around the last of '72 and beginning of '73, it snowed and I mean it snowed that year. Jeff was staying in this preacher named Cisroe Hunt's apartment so we went to church with him. He had a daughter that was about 15 years older than us and took a liking to us. Me and Jeff wind up getting Baptized at his Church, but we took it for a joke...we weren't serious. We were laughing and joking all through the Baptism.

We were Florida boys and got a chance to play in the snow, we stayed right on top of a hill. We would play football and slide down the hill tackling each other. While we were out playing around Rev. Hunt's car passed by with a girl driving it. An hour later Rev. Hunt made it home and was angry saying this gal he gave a ride stole his car while he was getting gas. We told him we knew where the car was and went with him to get it. When we caught up with the girl and car he put out a cursing on that young lady like the Pimps we knew in Miami. It was very funny.

I had Aunts in Atlanta, my mother's sister and my father's sister lived there. Now every now and then I tried to dress up in my Miami Spanish style suits with my platform shoes, but there were a lot more hills and pot holes in Atlanta, so I had to back down a little.

I came back to Daytona and there was nothing going on, so I went down to the Recruiting office and took the test. A few weeks after I went to MELPS. I talked with my brother and he okayed it for me to stay with him. I went to Lakeland and hung out with him for a while.

I heard later that Jimmie went back to Miami and was caught up in some deal with the Cubans and they trapped him in an alley and drove him into a wall killing him. Now that was the word that I heard. I never knew for sure. I do know that people was not afraid to kill you for the least little thing in Miami back in the day. If you weren't planning on moving on when you beat someone out of something you didn't hang around. Jimmie had this attitude like, "you will have to kill me". Maybe that's what they did. In your life, there will be some people you just want and need to put in your past and leave them there. It was deals that I saw go down and someone got beat, and the person showed up on the same set the next day. You supposed to let things cool down before you came back through but not Jimmie. Sometimes I would hear him arguing with these guys in Spanish, I didn't know what they were saying but I knew it wasn't good. He was good at threatening them that he would cut their throats, and I am sure he would have. He would say "nobody ain't gonna talk to me that way".

CHAPTER 6

When I got to Lakeland I was supposed to stay for just a few weeks. Me and my brother talked about it and we decided to share a 2-bed room apartment. I just had to find a way to come up with my part of the money. It was a nice apartment building with 4 units, 2 upstairs and 2 down stairs. It was located around a big lake on Magnolia Street. At the time my brother worked at Sunbeam Bakery and tried to get me a job there but at the time they were not hiring.

We used to party a lot, smoking our weed, THC, and other drugs, and drinking Miller Highlife beer. We would always go and buy the "Red hot sausage". "Playing Cisco Kid was a Friend of Mine." My brother's next door neighbor was a one-armed man name Monk; we called him one arm Monk. He was the director of Lakeland Recreation Department. At times, he would get moody when we played the music too loud and other times he was over partying with us. My brother was around 24 and I was about 19 years of age. Monk had a God Daughter that came over to see him a lot, but wind up over to our apartment most of the time. Monk would tell me that he didn't want me bothering his Goddaughter. After sometime passed he realized he couldn't stop me from seeing her. He knew that I was out of the streets and thought I was a slicker. He didn't want her to get hurt.

I would go out sometimes and come home and my brother would have his women and partying. One time I came in and he had this older lady, (between 55 to 60) older than our mother lying in the bed with no clothes on laughing and talking. It totally freaked me out. Now on the other hand, I was spending a lot of time with Monk's goddaughter Pinky, and he didn't like that. One day he came to me and said "if you are going to date my Goddaughter you got to get you a job".

That Monday he took me to Seaboard Coast Line Railroad to put in an application working as a crewman doing cleanups and fixing rails. Well, I noticed there were a lot of Blacks in the office already applying but no Whites. I ask the man at the desk why just blacks applying and no Whites and if this was the only thing that they were hiring for. He said no, there was another office down the hallway that was hiring Trainman, Switchman,

Conductors, and Engineers and he don't know why they don't ever go there and apply. I sensed that they were never told and never thought to ask. I left that office and went to the other office. It was empty except for myself. Every now and then a white guy would stop in. I asked the guy what did I have to do to get a Switchman Job, he told me all I needed was a high school degree, S.S. card, birth Cert. and get started. I didn't have none of that stuff with me so I had to catch the Greyhound Bus to Daytona Beach to pick-up all my paperwork.

    Now through all this time staying with my brother I was trying to change. I knew the life I was living had to change or I would be dead sooner than later. I was still getting high on a regular basis. A matter a fact I smoked a joint and took a hit of T.H.C. before I got on the bus. I would still pray and every now and then I would read the Bible high. I would sometimes find things in the bible that I could use to hustle people. The average woman was an easy target. Back in Daytona was my high school "sweet heart" with whom I had not officially broken up. And now in Lakeland I had another one but didn't care. I could handle it. When I got back to Daytona Beach it was the beginning of "Bike

Week" and I was high as a kite, but something was very different.

I was very uneasy for some reason. I just couldn't get right; a feeling came over me like it had never come over me before. I'd used these same drugs many times before but never felt like this. I got to my mother's house and went straight to my old bed room and locked the door, I fell to my knees before God and I prayed for several hours, I prayed and asked God to cleanse me and forgive me. I didn't want to be high anymore. It just didn't feel right that day and I wanted to be sober. Now normally that was a 12 to 14 hour high but the Lord Jesus cleansed my body and soul that day. This clean fluid began running from my nose until I was sober like I never been before. When I got off my knees I went right to my closet, I had a closet full of clothes that was tailored, shoes, suits, shirts and coats and if they didn't look like Christ I put them in the garbage. My neighbors were running to the garbage pulling clothes off the pile like "coming to America".

I knew that day God had visit me personally and overhauled my soul and changed my life at that moment. I began that day focusing on the spirit of God. The things I used to do, in a moment I couldn't do anymore. When I tried to do wrong, or think wrong, I felt guilt. I had a conscious and couldn't do it. That day I realized I had a Soul and I knew that I had to account for it. I knew that my soul was my treasure and God was holding it. I no longer questioned whether or not or if there was a God. Jesus is alive, and it's not just a story (fiction) but living, just waiting on us to call on him. The Lord was preparing me. He instructed my heart to Fast and Pray, to always acknowledging him I was learning to wait on him. I learned to not be so quick to speak and wait on the Lord Jesus to direct my path and control my tongue (putting words in my mouth).

Just that fast, I had become a stranger in my home and among my friends and family. My brother would say "Tony don't make a mockery of God" or "that's enough talking about God", almost wanting to fight. My mom had become a heavy drinker and kept plenty of Whiskey in the house. She always kept a couple of half Gallons in the cabinets. I know because I used to help her drink it. I was a heavy drinker in my early teens. When I drank the whiskey, I would replace it with water so she wouldn't find out. The legal age for drinking was 18 and I was a heavy drinker years before 18. I still had girlfriends in Atlanta, Miami, Daytona and ever where I went pretty much. That day I realized that I couldn't be this way anymore and right then and there I had to make a change. I talked to Toni my high school sweetheart, my friend in Atlanta, and the young woman in Lakeland. I got all my records and went back to Lakeland but came back changed.

My brother was business as usual smoking, drinking, and getting high. Now before I left Lakeland to get my papers, I had to take a physical for the railroad and I met this guy name Lewis who gave me and his brother-in- law a ride to take physical. We became good friends and I got back in touch with him when I returned. He seemed to know what I was going through when I told him my story about my new relationship with God, and how he changed me. I went by his house one day and met his wife and after talking with them both, we agreed to pray together. After praying they began to argue about something, I realized then that they were going through something too. Change is hard and once you decide to take a different path, a better path, obstacles will always present themselves. I knew that I had to find out how to maintain my relationship with God. I had too many things that I was still confronted with.

Lewis started hanging out with me and my brother. My brother would always speak with our neighbors above us, who just happen to be females. Of course, they liked us and would always make gestures about getting together. The girl that my brother was talking to had a boyfriend that was about 6ft. 8 and weighed about 350 lbs. One night the girls got the courage to come to our apartment. To show you how the devil works, Lewis challenged me about one of the other girls, about who would get her first. I accepted and in less than 5 minutes I had her in the bedroom undressing her. I won the bet and won in a record time. But unlike other times, I didn't feel good about this. I knew it was wrong. The boyfriend of the girl that my brother was talking to came up the stairs to the apartment and it sounded like he took 2 steps and was upstairs. Hearing him, we scrambled to get those girls out of the house before he found out. We got through that night without incident.

I was changing and more and more my conscious was bothering me but Lewis and my brother, every day they would party. The things I used to do I couldn't do any longer. I had heard a lot of the older people say this but now it was real in my life. For me and Beverly, Monk's goddaughter, she wanted things to stay the same, but I had changed and the change was too fast and too much for her. She wanted to be touched and I just couldn't do it. I started talking about waiting for marriage and she couldn't see that.

For the first time the Bible had a new meaning to my life and that was to live by it and learn more about God. Before I go on, I prayed daily and went back to the railroad that Monday. They gave me this big book and said this is "The Rail Road Bible. We live by it. We want you to read it and write in your own words what it means to you".

It took me a week to read it and write in my own words what it means. That Friday noon I turned it in, they reviewed it and that evening about 3 or 4 o'clock. They said, "Welcome to the railroad, you are hired." They issued me a brand new Accutron watch, the official railroad watch, a rules and regulation manual, lantern, and my own set of keys. I learned that when I "fast and pray" I understood the bible much clearer. I started fasting and praying 3 days at a time not drinking or eating. I would do this once a week. God had his anointing upon me and I could feel the trees, the water and all the nature around me. People started saying I was very strange.

My brother and Lewis would be getting high when I came home sometime and would say what's that glow about you. God was really blessing me. They knew that I was changing. As a person in the world I read the bible for self-gain, I knew most people trusted the Bible. This was the first time I had the anointing over me and read and understood in the spirit. It was such a great joy knowing that God cared enough for me and the whole world to let his "only son Jesus Christ "die on the Cross to save my soul. As a new babe in Christ I had to spread the good news. I no longer had to look over my shoulders in fear of someone coming to get me. I was not in a church when God saved me. He brought the Church to me. I knew that I needed to find a church to become a member of. So, I looked around and found "The Church of Our Lord Jesus Christ" Bishop Ross' church. I was doing well on my job but couldn't make as many services as I wanted to. So I worked for a few months and left got another job and started going to church more regular.

Through all this Beverly was falling out of love with me. She said I had lost my mind giving up a good job like that. I was a waiter at Morrison's Cafeteria but I was able to attend church more. I would get so high in the spirit that I would began shouting to the lord. This was common in a holiness church. My brother and Lewis began to be uncomfortable with me around, and his girlfriend and her sister moved back, so I decided to move. I moved in with one of the elder ladies of the church and a brother name McBride.

I remember one night it was "thundering and lighting and we were shouting to the sounds of the Thunder and lighting and Mother McIver said you boys better stop playing with the Lord and we replied we are not just enjoying God's work. She said "well I don't like that". Still a new babe in Christ I was in church with a lot of young saints and enjoying praising the lord shouting like King David. We would go on street corners spreading or pitch a tent spreading God words. When I lived in

Miami and Atlanta I would see men preaching in the middle of downtown, preaching on street corners. My thought was those guys are crazy. They were crazy in the Lord. I understood not being ashamed to tell people about Jesus. As time progressed I had forgotten that I had signed up for the military, my Recruiter reminded me. They came from Daytona Beach to get me. So eventually I went. Before I left I met a friend in Lakeland that I had met at Bethune Cookman he had similar experiences with Christ. His name was Clarence Bivens (Candy Man). Years later he was my Insurance man. While I was in Lakeland, that first guy I was supposed to fight when I first came to Daytona became one of my best friends and came to Lakeland to see me before I went into the military. (Gerald Murphy).

I went into the US Airforce, Lakeland Airforce Base in San Antonio, Texas. Now, I was a new Christian in Christ and was going into the military. When we got to the base we were called Rainbows with all the different colors. It was early in the morning, about 6am, with about a hundred new recruits going into the chaw hall and hearing about 300 to 400 hundred ball headed guys in green uniforms yelling "Rainbows" out to us. We spent Thanksgiving, Christmas and New Years' in boot camp. We couldn't look at T.V. until the Super Bowl came on and I was the only one from Florida in my whole Platoon. That was great but I hated being told what I could watch on T.V. It kind of turned me against watching football. Being in boot camp among so many troops and very few Christians became a problem and to make it I adjusted to fit in.

I could feel myself sliding backward and saying things that I knew were wrong and sometime doing things to fit in. We couldn't drink alcohol so we would go to sick call just to get cough syrup and get high off of it. I knew I was getting deeper and deeper and I tried to pick up some of my old way but it didn't feel the same. I knew that I was taking a chance but I knew better. God kept me even through my disobedience. One day while in boot camp, out of thousands upon thousands of solders on the biggest Military base in the world, San Antonio I looked over at the next squadron taking pictures and I told one of the guys "that look like one of my home boys". So, I walked over to him and said, "Julius Sessoms?" and he said, "Yak man

Tony. What in the world are you doing here." We both busted out laughing and said "out of all the people I ran into you". It was great. We hung out for a while but had to go back to our Squadron.

Back at the barracks was not so great. We had Squadron liberty but it was cancelled. We had a surprise inspection. Our T.I. had us line up and told us we did a great job in our inspection. We went back upstairs to our squadron and all the lockers was turned over. The beds were upside down, and our uniforms was everywhere. We were on restriction and was confined to the dorm having a G.I party. We had failed the inspection because of one person. There were 55 to 60 soldiers in our squadron and one person put socks in his laundry bag and left one drip of water in his canteen. We called him "Fife". We would always have to help him during inspection. He would always be the first one in the showers and the last one out. He would be sitting on the bench. This was brought to everyone attention. We found out that he was watching everyone take showers so we made him take showers by himself. Shortly after, he was sent back to his first day in boot camp.

Because we failed inspection, we would have to march everywhere grunting like a pig, oink, oink, oink, oink. I was the chow runner so I would have to march the squadron to chow. We would have to march in the chow hall heel to toe and no one really liked that. A black, Muscle bound guy name Peterson said when we got out of boot camp he would kick my behind, putting it nicely.

I went on to tech school in Wichita Falls, Texas. I took my briefcase and bible with me and while I was there, it came up missing. This base was large and I had no thought of ever finding it again. The airman's club was so big that they had 3 bands playing at one time. And every 3to 4 tables was fist fights. It was off the chain. The muscle bound black guy from New York who in boot camp that told me that he was going to get me was the first one I seen in the club. I just knew I would have to fight, but he was so glad to see me that he couldn't do nothing but hug me and shake my hand. He knew he needed as many friends as he could get. This was one fighting base.

All the barracks had beer machines with 5 or 6 different beers for 25 cents apiece. You could order a pizza and a 6pack of beer for $2.50. In the airman's club, you could eat a steak dinner for $1.25 and all the shots of whiskey were fifty cent. This made it so easy to sin and forget about being a good Christian.

There was a time that the blacks on the base fought for their own club. Segregation was new. When I finished, my specialty training we picked the base we wanted to go to on a dream sheet. My first choice was anywhere overseas. Second choice, anywhere up north. I got Montgomery, Alabama (Maxwell AFB). When I got to the base the guys asked me who was my supervisor and I told them Sgt. Audrey and they said to me, "man you got the worse supervisor on the base". The black and white guys was saying the same thing. Sergeant Audrey was a black, chubby, short guy that thought he was a ladies' man and you couldn't talk to him. He was married to a lady from Thailand and was always putting people down. He was very selfish. I was in supply and he made sure that I worked. This guy came from Thailand to cross train and he dressed in dress blues every day and I was all ways in combat gear. I got tired of it and bucked on him so he kept me in the commander's office. The guys had warned me so I started wearing my dress uniform and kicking back and I was back in front of the commander.

When I wasn't on duty I had started hanging out again with girls from the city. Also, I was seeing one of the officer's daughters. When I went into the military I started back talking with my high school sweet heart. She wrote me one day and said I think we should start seeing other people. When I read the letter, I knew something was wrong. I had bought a 1972 Grey Impala with the help of my mother, after I got stationed at the base. So, that weekend I got in my car drove all night from Maxwell AFB to Daytona Beach. This just added to problems that I was already going through. When I caught up with her she had already had a baby and was trying to hide from me. Over the years, I tried to talk to her but she wouldn't. It broke my heart that her life had changed and she was different person. She was a junior in college and just stopped going. (She had 2 more children later in life. After I got out of military I used to see her in the streets. Later in life she was the victim of a serial killer here in Daytona.)

I went back to Maxwell heartbroken that I had waited too late and I knew that it was on me.

Meantime I was still dealing with the base. My brother and sisters and a lot of first cousins were staying in Atlanta at the time and every other weekend I was going there to hang out. I went one weekend and left my car with my brother and caught the bus back. The next weekend coming back to Atlanta at the Greyhound bus station, I tried to pay a cab about 5am to take me to Decatur but no one would. I had a couple of half gallons of whiskey, and some 151 proof rum. Finally, one of the cab drivers said, "If you give me a drink of that rum, I'll give you a ride. I said there is no chaser, and he said I don't need one. Everyone warned him not to drink it straight. But he did and after drinking it he got worried and asked what I gave him. He told me to get in the cab and at gun point took me up the road and made me get out. He said "I better not ever see you again".

I made it to my brother's house and told him what had happened. At the end of that weekend I went back to base. Two weeks later I drove back to Atlanta. My brother didn't have a phone at the time so I drove to a gas station nearby to use the phone. The Decatur Police Department pulled up behind me and asked what I was doing. I told them I was calling my base (checking in). They asked me for my license. And I told them I didn't have them just my Military I.D. and the car registration which was in my name. I had a Florida license but had lost it when someone stole my briefcase. My brother's house was about 2 blocks down the hill and they wouldn't let him pick up my car. The Decatur Police arrested me and it cost me $300.00 dollars to get out of jail. They were a bunch of "Red Necks."

That Monday I went off duty and was going through it with my girl, so at the end of the week, Friday, I didn't go in for duty. That evening the Section Commander drove by and saw me walking. He stopped and asked me why I was not on duty. I told him I didn't feel like it. I had about an ounce of weed and a quart of Rum and I headed to Atlanta. On the way, I picked up a Hippie on the highway and a few miles later I picked-up 3 Black Guys that were broke down on the road. We smoked a little and I dropped them off about 30 or 40 miles down the road. Now me and the Hippie was still riding toward Atlanta and just crossing the Georgia / Alabama State line. We were getting high and laughing and talking when the police lights flashed on me. I looked down and I was driving over 90 miles an hour in a 55MPH speed zone. When he pulled me over the car was still full of smoke. He let me put the Hippie out and told me to follow him to the police station.

They arrested me because I was driving too fast over the speed limit and had to arrest me. They arrested me and impounded my car, never searching it. Grace and mercy...The guys were pretty cool even the jailer. I didn't have quite enough money to post bail and couldn't get in touch with none of my friends. That Monday I made a deal with the jailer. I sold him 2 Suede jackets and a Leather coat to get out of jail. I was walking in downtown LaGrange, Georgia and one of the G.I.s from the base lived there and bought me a ticket back to the base. A few days later, one of my buddies, James Parris, took me back to get my car.

When I went to see the Commander, he raised some sand and when me and another guy named Bear went to see the Commander, he was angry for the rest of the day. I was stuck in Alabama with a lot of civilians in my section and it didn't feel like the military. This base was a 3-year officer training base but I couldn't transfer so I wanted out. I got out of the military with an

Honorable Discharge and move to Atlanta. Before I left, they paid me all my back pay and gave me a slip from Sea Board Coastline Railroad to go back to work in Lakeland, Florida, but Lakeland was too slow so I wanted to live in Atlanta. I had forgotten that when I got the job on the railroad. I was already sworn into the military, so by law, they had to give me my job back.

I left Maxwell Air Force base about 2 am in the morning, after a private party. I had taken a hit of THC earlier. I had all my belongings packed away in my car headed to Atlanta. I drove 100 miles an hour for 100 miles up and down hills. I don't know why I wasn't killed. When I got to Atlanta the hood of my car was so hot that the paint was cracking.

The first place I stayed was with my cousin Barbara and her husband Lee. I stayed and later moved into my own studio apartment. My father visited me and stayed with me for a couple days. That was cool. I was around 21 or 22 at the time. Right after that, the maintenance man was doing work in my apartment and let someone steal all my stereo equipment. The apartment manager wouldn't replace my equipment so I moved with a guy that was friends with my sister. I moved into Boulder Crest Apartments with Charles and in a moment of bad judgement, I started dating his cousin. When we broke up he began acting nasty toward me. Go figure. I stayed long enough to find another place to live. Before I moved out, Charles was messing around with this girl who was living with another guy and almost got caught in their house. Charles brought the girl over to the apartment that night. The next morning I got up and the girl was there. About 7am someone was knocking at the door. We stayed on third floor with one way in and out. Charles had a little 22 pistol and a 22 rifle and asked me to take one. I refused. The guy kept knocking so Charles finally answered the door with the girl still in the room. This guy also had a gun on him and it was a 44 magnum.

Charles was trembling in his boots, and asked the girl to come out of the room. I had Charles put his gun down and I talked the guy back downstairs saying don't ruin your life for their wrongness. The guy had come to kill both of them and was hurt. I stood down stairs for a good while talking with the guy and he thanked me. I told him that I had been looking for another place to move. I wished him well and he went on. Shortly after this incident, I moved away.

The next place I stayed was with another Charles that had just got out of prison and when I moved in with him he had a stereo that looked just like mine. Charles loved walking around with a 357 magnum. I confronted him about the stereo and he swore up and down that it wasn't my stereo. I knew I couldn't stay in this place much longer.

I had found a job working with my brother at Clean Rate Cleaners. They pre-washed all kind of Jeans for "Male Blue Jean". I had about 30 or 40 different jean outfits turned up missing. I looked in his room and they were in his closet.

At the time, I was dating this older girl that had 2 daughters and she was the only child. We went out one day and her mother died in her sleep after we all had been drinking together. It was hard times, Ford was President and we had been debating about him. I had moved in with them and we couldn't pay the electric bill so I put a wire in the meter and put the cap back on. It worked for as long as we needed it.

After the funeral, we found an apartment together off of Cascade and Gordon Road. We found out she was pregnant and since she was by herself with 2 children, we moved in together. She had a 1967 blue GTO with a black top. During the 3rd to 4th month of her pregnancy, she lost the baby so when we got on our feet I made a move and thought it was time to leave Atlanta. Prior to staying with her, I went to school at DeKalb College, majoring in Music Theory. I came back to Daytona and stayed with my mom for a while. I stayed in and out of relationships and started hanging out with Baby brother an old friend of my brother's and 1st cousin Bra Shake. Baby Brother was the best Drummer in Central Florida and played behind a lot of famous groups. My cousin had mentioned him earlier and said he could help me with my music so I hooked up with him and when he wasn't on the road we were working at his father Paint and Body Shop.

We used to call his father General because he was high into the Free Masons and was a good man. Baby Bra had 5 brothers and 3 sisters and I was considered the 7th brother. When the older musicians played on sets they would always go and light up before they went on stage. For a few years, I tried to play keyboards. When Oz (Smut got out of jail); he would play base and lead guitar. Paul would pull out his Gibson guitar. Sometimes Berry would come by. They would close the paint shop down early and practice. Charles Akins, Johnny Logan and a lot of other Musicians would just come by and just do a set. People would always be hanging around. Aaron played with the Almond Brothers and Greg used to come by a lot when he was in town.

I liked this girl that had a green LTD and she used to come by and pick me up. She was about 6' 2" and they called her "the Amazon" and it looked funny when I was with her, like I was her little boy. Baby Bro and his wife, Mrs. Watson, gave birth to another daughter and named me as one of the three godfathers. He said he did it that way in case one don't act right. Now back to Amazon. We went horseback riding off Tomoka Farm Road: her, myself and her male, first cousin. They gave all three of us a horse. They gave her a big "White Stallion" and gave us what looked like two Donkeys. They were galloping all over the woods and mine wouldn't move and every time I tried to make him he would turn around and try to bite me. That was a crazy day; I remember feeling like a mistreated little child.

I was turning 23 to 24 years of age, and knew I needed to find a career so I started working at the police department as a maintenance man, taking the trustees around police station and substation, watching them clean up. This was through the Cedar Program. That way they could hire you for six months without benefits and let you go for 2 months and then hire you back for another six months. They did this for a few years. Even the Fire Dept. hired Black fireman the same way.

In 1978 I had to make a decision whether I wanted to be a Policeman or Fireman after much thought I decided to be a Fireman. I didn't feel right being a Policeman because I would have to arrest too many of my friends. In 1979 I became a full-time Daytona Beach Fireman.

CHAPTER 7

Now the fire department had Black firemen but they were hired mostly through the CETA Program, a temporary work program that worked you for 6 months at a time and lay you off for about 2 months and then hire you back). This way, they didn't have to hire you permanently. If not for this program, there would be few or no blacks in the fire department. 1979 was the first year that firemen had to be state certified. I was in one of 2 of the first classes.

Of all the hard times, I went through and took myself through I was glad to be back in a paramilitary organization. I often times wished I would have stayed in the "Air Force" for 20 years. In the fire department, we trained for the state test and most of us, if not, all of us, passed the state certification the first time. Most of the instructors at firemen school, E.M.T school, was Daytona Beach firemen. From my past life, how I lived I was in this position only by "God's" grace and mercy. My life could have gone either way. I know I could have been dead or in prison. I didn't see either. Instead I was doing this, I saw so many of my friends go to jail, get killed or still living in the past.

I know that if you believe in yourself that there is nothing that you cannot do if you believe. This was something that I wanted to do and I was proud of it. I finally got a chance to give back and it felt great. It wasn't easy finding myself, but glory be to God he held a place for my life. When you get the urge to give up, try even harder. Make the devil out of a liar. It may even take you longer than others to accomplish your goal or goals, just don't give up. I learned that most of the time, it's that extra little push that takes you over.

These was the time of "Urban Renewal" they were buying out homes and tearing the building down and building big business. They were building larger Hotels and most of the time the land owner was getting less than what the property was worth. That meant that a lot of people was burning their houses and business down for the insurance money. The firefighter business was booming it was a lot of work for everyone.

For a few years, we had at least 3 "Big Fires" a night. We could stand at the stations and see the fires from the stations. When I came on "Fireman stood on the tailboards" (the very rear of the fire engine and Otis was a senior fireman, he had been on for 23+ years. On the way to the fires he would be standing on the tailboard smoking a black Jack Cigar all the way to the fire. One time when I needed him backing me up he was still outside gearing up. Otis was obese and out of shape, and it took him longer to gear up. I was sent up to the third floor of this building with 1 1/2" line and was told all the power was out, but it wasn't. I could feel an electrical charge through the hand line and my turn-out boots. You weren't supposed to go in until the power was off in a fully involved structure fire. With the entire building water logged, the floor we were standing on gave way and we almost fell to the next floor.

In most structure fires, you can't see your hands in front of you, it's like being blind and feeling your way to put out the fires or do search and rescue. Your first fire is called "Getting your Cherry Busted."

Death by fire is not a pretty sight. We found this one lady in the kitchen at her refrigerator, her skin appeared to be melted and she looked like a doll crying blood. Needless to say, she was dead. A lot of times, we would work all night at fires, and be released from the streets by the next crew.

A few months later that same year, I got my first fire death where I actually saw the victim in the act of getting burned. He was a white male, in his early 40s, that just had retired from the Navy. He had been drinking and fell asleep smoking. We got a fire call stating that they had a "structure fire "at 411 North Halifax, which was about a 100-unit apartment complex. We had to go door to door to find out which unit was on fire. Now me, being a young fireman, didn't want to be the one to find it but as fate would have it, I found it first. I felt the door with the back of my hand and it was hot to the touch. I kicked the door in and called for backup.

It was crazy. You couldn't see any smoke or tell the apartment was on fire from the outside, but now I could see the man running around in flames, screaming help me somebody, so I had my 11/2 line charged and extinguished the fire with a water fog. When we found the man in the burned rubble he looked at me and said "man I think I messed up this time." He had 3rd degree burns all over his body. He was a White male but he was black as coals. He died a few hours later. Jack was the Paramedic on the scene.

During this time over the years it was common to kick a door in finding drunks asleep with pots on the stove with the kitchen on fire, after coming from clubs late at night. We had a call on an elderly white male that had been missing for several days. His relatives were trying to get in contact with him. We went to his appointment, and knocked on the door and no one answered but we noticed in the window on the inside were thousands and thousands of flies just sitting there. We gained entry through the back door and the odor was so bad that we couldn't just walk in. We had to gear up in turnout gear (fire suit) to go in. We found the man at the front door and he had been dead for several days. He was almost total consumed by maggots and flies.

Over the years, I've had similar calls, finding people dead in their beds for several days. Most of the time, they swell up and would be about to burst.

From 1983 and beyond there were a lot of bad scenes because of "Drug Shootouts". There were a lot of murders from robbing drug houses and drug dealers. Sometimes the dealers were hiring hit men to take the guys out that was doing the robbing. We would go through some of the houses and see thousands of dollars and drugs with blood and bodies all over the house. We would go in searching for victims. We have had some that ran to the rescue truck to get treated. I remember one night we got a call for injured person and the dispatcher said it location was just west of the police station.

When we arrived on the fire engine it was a very cold night, we searched around the area finding a young female, half nude lying in a pool of her own blood in the freezing cold. No policeman nowhere. This was right across the street from the police station. In shock, (disbelief), a four-man crew froze for a moment. We found out someone had raped her and threw her out of the car and left her for dead.

1984 I was a new Paramedic and there were a lot of murders and suicides on a regular basis. Even elderly people was committing suicide. One night we had 3 different incidents with people getting their throats cut at different bars within 45minutes. We had 2 suicides within 30 minutes of each other 2 streets over. Now Bike week was always a lot of tension.

Being a new Paramedic the night before "Bike Week" we got a call that a wine-o had stabbed another Wine-o in the butt over a bottle of wine. He had a huge hematoma on his butt. We joked and laughed about that until we were soaking wet. About 2am that morning we got a 911 call stating "We need 2 unit's. A lady was cut in half". We pulled up on the scene thinking that it was just a practice drill. It didn't look real. I told my partner that this was some drill. He said this was a fu--in joke. P.D. ran to the truck and said I think one is still living. We walked up to the victims and half of a white female Blonde hair was lying face up with eyes wide open gritting her teeth and all the meat peeled off her spine. The other half of her body was about 20 feet away lying on her stomach with all her insides lying out. Her legs were straight and locked. In the middle of her was a white male against the post and was broken up and couldn't move.

That week we got several other Motorcycle deaths. We had sometimes guys with both legs and arms broken and this was a normal call on motorcycle weeks. We had a young white male on a motorcycle that was trying to go around a car on Main Street Bridge and was caught between two cars. The two cars split him down the middle. It was like someone was making a wish. By now, I was on a lot of bad calls but the girl that was cut in half, touched me the most. It didn't get to me to sometime later. I had a lot of nightmares behind it.

Moving on we had to standby on man hunts when shooter was still on the scene. I went in one time behind one of the detectives, feeling the power, and was told to get out, what was I gonna shot with my drug box. We were getting to use to the action. One time I got a 911 call (a black male having chest pains) when I arrived on the scene I found out it was my first cousin, it caught me off guard because I didn't know until that day that he had heart problems. A few years later he died. Now while we were at the funeral, my brother was standing outside the church crying and cursing and swearing out loud. God damn, etc. I walked out of the church to try to get him to calm down and he said out loud, "Tony don't come out here fucking with me. He was drunk but most of the time this was his way. He had reenlisted in the military and had moved to Warner Robbins AFB in Georgia.

In 1986 I met my wife to be. At the time, she was working at Eckerd's drugs store and I was developing some pictures. I took pictures for weddings, birthdays, college girls, etc., for a side job. During this period, I was involved with a lot of women and not really thinking about settling down. I had resigned from the fire dept. because I was burned out (no pun intended). Right after we started dating, my partner Terry left to play for the Jets but I was still running with two other guys that used to play pro ball. On my birthday, they threw me a birthday party and the theme song was "JAIL BAIT". There were about thirteen to fourteen girls and three males. I was really enjoying my life but I also really liked Irish.

I had been dating her for a little while, and I thought she was getting a little bossy, so we were off and on. As time went on I knew I needed to stabilize so I decided to go back to the fire department after being off for 3 ½ months. They hired me right back, I believe mainly because they needed some more black firemen and I was already certified. The chief asked me why did I want to come back I replied, jokingly, "I need a part time job". The assistant chief shook his head "no" behind the chief's back. Tony will always be Tony.

Irish and I were doing pretty good and we were very intimate so guess what...the next year our first son Tony Jr. was born on my birthday and I delivered him. The following year we had Malcolm in Sept. and on December 30th we were married by Rev. Yorker. Terry was my best man. We decided that we needed to put some order to the chaos.

Making kids and not being married didn't feel right. In our marriage, we had some hard times. I knew that I would go through some things so I kept reaping what I had sowed. The Bible had warned me. We went on to have another son Jonathan. My two older boys named him from the Bible story that my wife had read to them, David soul mate. Life had its up and downs but we kept living and making mistakes.

In and around 1994 my wife and kids started going to church. Now I was glad because we were out to the school 2 to 3times a week dealing with Tony. Nothing seemed to work. They would always ask daddy are you going to church with us today and I would say you all go and pray for me. I had worked all night and wanted to relax. One Sunday they asked me and I couldn't say no because God was speaking to my heart saying if you don't get out of that bed this may be your last chance. So I went to church. After a few Sunday Tony Jr. wanted to join the church and I stopped him, and he started a second time and I stopped him again the third time I let him go and went up with him. My other two boys followed us up. So me and our 3 sons joined the church that day. A Sunday or two after my wife joined the church.

In 1996, we got a call that my dad was dying of leukemia and was in the V.A. hospital in East Orange, New Jersey. We planned and took the trip. With my wife and kids, we went through Savannah to pick up my brother. I drove through North and South Carolina and into Virginia but when I got to Richman I was driving in the middle of the bridge and my brother started laughing saying he's scared of bridges. As I drove further he noticed I was driving slow and said "boy you drive like a old man". I was very uncomfortable so he took over driving.

He was used to driving all over the states because his job in the military sent him all over the country and he loved to drive. He was on the Jersey Turn Pike going around people with Jersey and New York tags. He drove fast and I was hanging on. We made it their safe and was greeted by our little brother John. I had met John for the first time and he was the same age as my wife. We found out they were born on the very same day. We also met my sister Sherri's two daughters, Angelica and Anya and her son, Admere. Sherri died around 1989 on Mother's Day delivering her last child. She went into a coma and never came out of it.

    My sisters were smart to fly into New Jersey. It was great spending time with my dad, brother and the rest of the family. I found my little brother John to be a wonderful lil' brother. I was a big brother and he looked up to me. Jersey as a city had some rough spots but over all, it was beautiful. On the way back from Jersey, Irish and I were exchanging some words so my big brother decided he would straighten me out. Half way from New Jersey we were arguing and he began to talk about how hard he had it and what he had to go through and all the tough times. I told him my story and I think we both were surprised about somethings that happened. When we got back to Savannah we had little to say to one another. He didn't go back to his house. He went to his new girlfriend Shelia's house. I think the words were "I'll see you later".

Later that year, around Dec 1997 my father died. I was on duty at the Fire Department in the middle of a lightning storm and all the units in Daytona were out on calls. Some calls were still backed up and being held for the next available unit. We got a call from an elderly female having chest pains. In the middle of the call we got a call on the fire engine phone and it was to tell me that my father had died. The crew could only look at each other in disbelief saying "are they out of their mind".

We cleared the chest pain and the dispatcher gave us the next call, a possible suicide. The crew asked was I O.K. and wanted to give the call to another unit but I agreed to go on. Upon arrival, we saw a girl that lived in the apartments and she told us that her neighbor next door left a note on her door saying that there was a dead man next door. We entered the house and found it was clean from top to bottom. We went into the bathroom and saw an 80-year-old man in the bath tub with a 357

Magnum in his mouth and his brains splattered all over the ceiling. I made it through that day.

A few days later, we rented a van in Florida, picked up my brother Andrew, and drove to New Jersey for the funeral. My fathers' hair was curly and grey all over and because of his illness he hardly looked like himself. We were glad that we had spent time with him before he died. In spite of everything, he was still our dad.

Andrew and I didn't argue this time. We kind of stayed out of each other way. We did share a room in Jersey and as time passed we began to make amends. When he returned home, my brother started going to church and would call quite often, or I would call him.

In August 20, 1998, my beautiful daughter Sherri was born and I was still working for the Fire Department and in the year of the "Big brush fires" These were some of the worst brush fires that the state of Florida had ever experienced in my life time and beyond.

Sherri was named after my wife's and my sister. We both have sisters name Sherri. All of our children were beautiful, but Sherri (WOW) she was breath takingly B_E_A_U_T_I_F_U_L!! I asked my crew, Bruce and John and their wives to be Sherri's God parents along with Cassandra from church. Sherri had plenty of God parents because we wanted to make sure that she would always know she was loved.

When I was off duty during the time of the "Florida Brush Fires" I got a 2 day leave and we went to Tampa to get away from the smoke with the new baby. In the "1998 Brush Fires" I was a Driver Engineer for station#4 and me, Bruce and John were a crew. While in route to fight the fires, we looked at each other and started laughing out loud. We knew we were in for a time. We were driving through Ormond Beach with burning buildings on each side of the highway. Businesses was burning, "electrical poles" were all over the roadway. We went to Flagler County for mutual aid. Every city we passed through had burning buildings but in Daytona Beach, we did not lose one building. In most cases, we stopped the fire right at the door.

Our motto was the buck stop here. We had firefighters from all over the world fighting side by side with us, some didn't speak English. Some flew in from the Middle East Oil fires. If you've never seen a wild Brush Fire, it leaves nothing living or standing in its path. (It reminds you of Death Valley). After the brush fires, Disney and most of the theme parks gave firefighters and their friends and family free passes to the parks for over a year. We were "Theme Parked out" after that. Now during the "Fires people from all over was coming by the stations with all kinds of supplies, change of underclothes, cases of gator aid, drinks etc. The stations bay floors were so full of supplies that we had to park the Fire Engines outside. Over several weeks things got back to normal and I was finally getting my brother back.

    Andrew kept in contact with me all through the brush fires making sure that the family was okay. On October 10, 1999, my brother got married and asked me to be his best man. Man, being my brother's best man was great. This was also on my brother's birthday. Around the year 2000, when he called and talked, it was always about what he wanted to do for his children. He would come home a lot and him and his wife Shelia would stay with my mom. He always fell asleep in that same recliner when he was home.

    Andrew told us later that year that he had cancer. This was a shock to the family. On top of this a few months later, June 2001, my brother-in-law Lewis lost his "twin sister Lois". Now my brother wouldn't tell us for a while about his sickness and we wondered how long he knew he had cancer. He didn't want us to worry. His cancer got worse and they sent him to the military hospital in Augusta, Georgia.

When we went to see him, his curly black hair had turned fully grey, just like my father. Every other week I tried to drive up to be with his. I hated seeing him suffering. They continued giving him treatment and trying everything they could but eventually they gave up. They took him back to Savannah and put him in the hospital there and then in hospice. My brother went to sleep on August 29, 2001 but before he did he had given his life to Christ. He had served over 28 years in the Military. I still to this day get the urge to call him.

Now, I am about 14 years older that my wife. Our friends use to tease me by saying that I use to drive the fire truck by the nursery while she was in the playground and say that's gonna be my wife one day. I knew it was all in fun.

Now in January 2000, I lost my two next door neighbors, one to gunshots and the other for shooting him. The one doing the shooting had Alzheimer and the disease affected his mind to the point that he shot the other. I am sure that he would never have done this in his right mind.

That morning, I was warming my car up before going on duty. I put the car seat in the car for my baby daughter. When I step back in the house to get my daughter, I heard two gun shots. A few seconds later, it could have been me or me and my daughter. Now this was getting too close to home. My neighbor had been shot. I held my neighbor until emergency truck came and told his daughter that he was going to be alright but he wasn't alright. We lost them both this day. We would all ways exchange Christmas gift and eat together every year. We would even get together and pray for the neighborhood. Things were changing and I decided to retire shortly after.

I took about a month vacation and retired while on vacation. About the middle of February, I got a call from my sister telling me that they had a man hunt for my nephew. He was wanted dead or alive. Well, this frightened me. I felt that he would come by my house. I was home with my newborn daughter and I didn't want him in the house. Just as I expected, he came by my house. I wouldn't let him inside in fear that U.S. Marshalls would have a shootout in my yard or house. I let him use my cordless phone outside and he left. It wasn't ten minutes later that I looked out of the windows and saw that local policemen, U.S. Marshalls and other law enforcement agencies had my house surrounded with all type of assault rifles. They were coming out of the woods from the back yard. I began screaming to the top of my voice "there is no one here but me and my baby daughter". They replied come out with your hands up, and I came out with my daughter in my hands a bit shaken. After the search, they apologized and the U.S. Marshall congratulated me on my retirement. I had met him several times before on 911 calls and knew most of local policeman. They stated they had to make sure I wasn't being held hostage.

In March of 2000, I was the first African American to retire from Daytona Beach Fire Department. When I retired, I went straight to The Department of Juvenile Justice and it became a ministry.

CHAPTER 8

God blessed me to pray and witness to the youth in custody. I had to deal with kids from broken homes and a lot of their parents were in prison or had been in prison. Some didn't believe in God and worshipped the devil. These kids would cut themselves and consecrate the bible with blood. We had some kids that would take their #2(fecal) and spread it all over the windows and walls. We had kid that was on suicide watch, sometimes 15 to 20 at a time. The sad part about it is, a lot of these kids came from good homes and committed these crimes because they were bored.

Kids were in for major felonies, murders, strong-arm robbery, carjacking, home invasions and a lot of other crimes. And a lot of the kids that was committing these crimes was 13 and 14 years of age. We had kids that was breaking each other jaws and arms in custody. As you know, by now I was getting older, and when the all call for "available staff to an area in the compound" we responded to that area. Sometimes it was two individuals on a group against another group or a group gang banging one or more individuals. The girls were just as violent as the boys. Sometimes you had to take a fall to keep the youth or others from getting severe injuries. The kids would use plastic spoons, pencils and other contrabands for weapons. We had kids that were one on one 24 hrs. A day 7 days a week. That meant that there had to be a person assigned to watch them around the clock. This normally tied up one staff per shift. We had kids sometime 15 to 20 at a time you had to watch and never take your eye off.

The regular kids you watch all the time but when they were in their rooms we did 10 minute checks but sight and sound kids you couldn't take your eyes off them even in the toilet. Kids would commit these violent crimes and when some went to court and got sentenced they would act surprised.

Some of the kids would say things like "I can't go to a program" and would threaten other youth or sometimes the staff. They would even try to do something to get them transported to adult jail, aggravated battery and other crimes on other youth or staff. Most of the time, if we felt we were about to have a problem, we would have an extra unit standing by and would have a team standing by at intake at the jail. Everything that you did was on camera and you had to do everything by the book, because everything you did had to be in your written report. If they reviewed the camera and it wasn't in the report you were investigated and put on no client contact.

Now the youth that you had to deal with could call abuse and administration would put you on no client contact until after the investigation. The kids had more rights than the staff, you were guilty until proven innocent. The problem was with the younger staff is that they took things to heart when the youth acted out against them.

Most of the time when a kid went to trial he would be ready to hurt anyone that stood in his was or in his sight. They would say I want to be adjudicated to an adult so I can bond out, he would look for someone to assault. We tried to prepare for kid like this by taking him to another detention until his bed open. Most of the time, kids in leg irons and handcuffs would fight the staff all the way to the next location and try to kick the windows out trying to escape. Sometimes crashing windows while on the interstates. At times, we traveled 100 plus miles transporting these youths. After dealing with these kinds of problems at work (Jail), it would make me appreciate coming home to my wife and children. I worked for 8 plus years with Juvenile Justice and retired in 2008.

In June 2003, my brother-in-law Lewis almost lost his life to a train wreck. A dump truck ran into the train pending Lewis against the train and the dump truck over 2 hrs. It took them to free him up. He was in a coma for 4 weeks. When he came out of it he said he was walking around his home town with some lady, the whole time he was out. Lewis lost one of his legs and have just partial use of the other one but it brought him closer to God.

He acknowledged him now. Lewis said that during the two hours that he was pent against that train, he never lost consciousness, and the first things that the paramedics said upon arrival was that the patient has an amputee. Both legs up to the thighs are amputated. He said he remembered saying out loud "I lost both of my legs" and then he passed out.

My wife's mother, Rolene, had been fighting cancer for about 15 years. She refused to take treatments and said she would wait on the lord. The doctor had given her a little over a year to live, but she lived 14 years longer than they gave her. While I was still on the fire department, she would call 911 for shortness of breath or other medical problems sometimes. Whoever responded would call me. One time she got fish juice in her eyes she said. Well, I use to tease her about wanting to see some of the young men on the fire department. In the year 2008 on December 20th, while we were there at the hospital (Most of her family), she took her last breath and went to sleep. She lived about 15 years longer than the doctors had given her. She would not take chemotherapy. She trusted in God taking care of her.

Even though I have made a lot of mistakes in my life, I know God have forgiven me over and over again. There were too many times that I should have been dead but I'm still here. A lot of my friends, as well as my enemies, have fallen but God has kept me here. My hope is that God blesses my friends and my enemies, my family and my extended family.

Now who am I? I am a continuous work of God how he brought me from the lowest of lows into a blessing for myself and others. I am a doubter made into a believer, a hater to a lover, troubled person to a peaceful person, a vengeful person to a forgiving person, a non-believer to a believer, and a teaser to a praiser.

I feared God from the beginning, when I was a child and my family was in trouble but he showed me even then he was there with a plan. Look what he did. He blessed every one of my sisters and brothers and put it in all our hearts to continue loving our father. He put it in our hearts to not point the finger but reach out our hands to our brother imperfections that they may reach out as well. Isn't God wonderful? He's never too busy to talk. He's never too busy to just let you say just what's on your heart. Ain't he wonderful! He promises you everything and asks for nothing in return. Ain't God great? Who am I, I am waiting to see. I will wait on the Lord to surprise my heart.

Our last son Marcus was born on Feb 26 2003. We were in Augusta, Georgia visiting my sister in law Marlene when the doctor called Irish and told her that she was pregnant. When she told me I almost fell out of my chair. She looked at me and said "are you not happy?" I replied "yes but you caught me off guard". This was the day before the 4th of July, which was Tony's and my birthday. We decided to name him Marcus Andrew after my brother, so Marcus and my brother have the same middle name.

I was engaged several times in my life but it didn't happen. I was 34 when I had my first child on my birthday. Now I have 5, the last one at the age of 50. Who said that God don't have a sense of humor? There were times when all I had was my word yet God has filled my life with great joy and a legacy of wonderful children and grandchildren. God has shown himself to me in times of great struggle as well.

One time was when my wife was pregnant with our child before Jonathan, she had a miscarriage. We lost our son the same day I was to start a new part time job with Tyrone. I went to the hospital with my wife, and Tyrone didn't believe me. After that, Tyrone, his wife Michelle and their family became one of our dearest friends. We have been neighbors in a praying neighborhood for many years. Over 20 years ago, Terry and I had planned to live next door to each other in a different neighborhood and it didn't happen. But in 2003 we were closing on houses in the same neighborhood and next door to each other. Neither one knew the other was buying their homes. Mr. Williams, another neighbor, lived in the same area in Hastings and at a younger age was a migrant worker in the same camps that my family worked in a few years earlier. It is amazing that God puts people in your life and brings joy when at one time there was pain. There are no coincidences. I grew up with the brother of my neighbor on the right side of me and he grew up with my wife. Even in my church there are families that we hold dear to our hearts. We know that God truly has his hand on their families. I can say a lot of good things happened in my life.

In 1985, my mother met a man named Fletcher Little at a Masons' convention in Chicago. He became my stepfather. He was a past Grand Master of Chicago. He had a townhouse home in Champaign, Illinois and my mother had a home here in Florida. They used to travel back and forth about 3 to 4 times a year. He was a great man. I was happy for my mother because she was finally truly happy. Fletcher always responded to mom with "yes baby", "okay baby" and never raised his voice. He was better than my own father was to my mother even though they had 6 children together. I remember, one year before my dad died, he came to Daytona to visit and he and Fletcher sat around talking like they had known each other all their lives. Papa Fletcher died in 2003 he was 97 years old. My mother took his body back to Chicago.

CHAPTER 9

Take a stand for your life daily. Learn to be patient leaning on Jesus, but be active while you Wait. Knowing that the Lord Jesus knows your needs better than we do. It's not always about you, (you may be someone's "Angel in the time of need). Let God use you.

Always remember to love mightily and forgive with all your heart. Take the burdens off you and give them to God. Continue Praying instead of guessing or trying to figure someone out. Truly loving your enemies even when you are clearly mistreated, or misunderstood heals you and allows you to grow even closer to God. Hate only destroys the hater.

What might not be clear to you, is seen very clearly through God's eyes. Normally confusion is the "evil ones" way of trying to steal your joy or make you miss your blessing.

Breathing in air cannot be seen but felt, and you know that you need it to live. You feel God with your heart and soul and you need Him to live eternally. This is His promise to all of us for believing in Him. Just like the air you breathe, you can't see Him but you can feel his presence. Trust in the true presence of God.

I've learned in life, even when things are perfectly calm, "Storms" pop up every now and then. The best was to ride a storm is be at peace, be still, and listen with your heart and soul.

When you are confronted wait, instead of blowing up, God might have sent them with a word to calm you down. My hope and dream is that someone will learn from my life and know that you can get control of your situation and turn it to good. I learned to not depend on my own wisdom but to depend on God. I have been forgiven many times in my life. I have made a great deal of mistakes. I'm just glad that I know that if you ask God for forgiveness with a sincere heart he will forgive you as many times you ask for forgiveness.

Ever child that is born in this world deserves to be loved. They deserve attention, and to know how they feel is important. With all my heart, I wish God to guide and protect their beautiful spirits. The world needs to know that there are millions and millions of children unwanted by their parents. Some of the cases I witnessed in the court room made me hold my breath to keep from crying during trails. Sometimes all a child needs are kind words. Just letting a child or adult know you care can make a positive difference in their life. It is a great feeling when a kid that I dealt with in detention comes up to me and says "thanks, I am doing great and this is my fiancée." To see one working in some business or to see one in church or in college, in the military, or to say this is my child or children is confirmation that God hears our prayers and answers.

I retired but kids that are now adults still come to me all the time with such great news. It's the ones that don't learn that bother you. I hear about some that go to prison or get killed in the act of committing a crime. Kids killing kids. God bless our Children. Bless our world, keep us safe. Strengthen our children, open their minds to make good choices.

I know how easy it is for a man to live in the world and become old and never truly become a man in mind and spirit, taking this beating to the grave. Be true to yourself, having a God filled life is not easy. If it was, everyone would have it. You must be willing to give of yourself what is needed to become who you are in heart. Do your best, even when people are not pleased, God will be. Don't worry about people, worry about if God is pleased, be true to yourself. Explore your options don't give up.

I know how easy it is to give up, I have many of times. I had to start believing in myself. Confidence in the promises of God made it much easier. When you walk through life walk in peace, be encouraged by a good word and always leave a good word to encourage others. Learn to forgive and not take everything to heart when done or treated wrongfully. Pray for the storms or trouble in your brother's life to calm.

Now to show you how God works, one of my friends from the Fire Department, Frank, has a son that's a teenager around 17 years of age. He was rebellious and was to the point of fighting his dad. To be exact he did fight his dad and broke several appliances around the house. Frank and his wife are both God-fearing but they were to the point of sending their son to a commitment program. Frank felt his back was against the wall and didn't want his son to go to prison for some of the things he was doing or was about to do. His son was hanging around the wrong crowd. Some of the boys' names I knew from working in the system. I had the opportunity to talk to Frank and he agreed to me setting up a visit to a Judge that was a friend of mine (Judge Grimes). The Judge also agreed to it.

On the way to court, I had a chance to talk to Junior, Frank's son. His attitude was evident in the anger he expressed and he wanted to hurt someone. He loved fighting. When we got to court, the Judge invited us up front in the jury stand. Everyone in court noticed his demeanor appeared to be a time bomb just waiting to go off. This judge had several juveniles on trial and Jr. had a chance to see the consequences of their actions. I think what was going on in court kind of hit home. When he heard about the years of imprisonment that they were faced with it held is attention and made him very emotional. The Judge requested that Jr. hang around until after court because he wanted to talk to him. Judge Grimes called Junior up to the bench and when he approached him one of the kids in custody requested to speak to Junior. Judge Grimes allowed the kids in custody to tell him how they had to live in jail and how they had to sleep on concrete slabs, with their roommate sitting on the toilet, and the water fountain over the toilet. These kids could tell him better than anybody else could tell him, because they saw themselves in Junior. The good thing was that Jr. appeared to be listening. Judge Grimes talked to him about his demeanor and how he had many of children with similar attitudes who were either dead or in prison. Now all the time the Judge was talking to Jr., he would not look up.

The judge told him that he never wanted to see him look down when anyone was talking to him but look them straight in their eyes. He said not down or up but straight in their eyes. After leaving the court room Frank stated that Jr. had never talked as much as he did on the way home. Frank called and told me Jr. was going to church with his mother and when he talked to other people he always looked them straight in the eyes. Every now and then I called and sometimes Jr. had a small problem but got it back in control. Sometime later I talked to a common friend of me and Frank and the first thing he said to me was "Have you seen Frank's son lately? I love the way he looks you straight in the eyes and talks to you. I love that in a young man. Now that was far better than having to send him away to some program. Believe me it works when you put all things in God's hand.

A man threatened me while holding a gun behind his back years ago. In the mist of writing my book, I had a chance to remind him of this incident at an outing that we were both invited to attend. We laughed about it and gave each other a Holy hug. I know he was the same person in body, but truly not in spirit. I feel that everyone that has lived on this earth has a story to tell. As a dear friend always says "we all got stuff, some just more than others."

During 2008, in my life time, a black President was voted into office (Barrack Obama). It was a time that we all hoped that America was maturing. My mother and other older people got to see this in their life time. The world took notice of this and applauded America.

In Dec. 2009 for the first time during a retirement party for Bruce and Frank from the Fire Dept., The Precise Brother Hood an organization of Black Firefighters hosted a party for them. As a member of this organization, it made me feel great knowing that now about 30% of the department is African American. And at least 75% of them are

Engineers and Lieutenants. When I was on the Department there were only about 8% blacks at the most. Looking at these guys I know we are blessed and we can succeed trusting in the Lord.

God is busy, his hand is everywhere. My mother turned 89 this year but so many others were not able to witness this. And as far as our children everything seem to multiply many times over. Needless deaths after deaths, so many broken hearts. Lord keep our children safe we try as parents but you have all things in your hands. Lord keep our children. I will continually leave my doors open for my remakes through The Lord Jesus Christ. They say, (meaning the "old timers) that you never stop working. You work until the day you die.

You would hope that you can lay back and enjoy life. The only thing is having children or just friends or family, oh even strangers, the art or spirit of giving comes with great power. Learning how to give is a job within itself. It's hard to give someone your last, it's hard to stop and help someone when you are in a hurry, and it's hard to give your all when you don't feel like it.

Oh, but the older I get the more I realize that giving your all in everything you do no matter how large or small is worth the effort. Whether at work, home, or where ever it is, giving your all is like "a treasure chest of Gold." Who don't like gold?

This is how you have to present yourself to the world, like gold, your inner and outer self, from core to core, bright and shiny.

No one wants "a treasure chest full of rocks or any other worthless weight, something to slow them down. They want that spirit of gold. Look at your life as being that "Treasure chest of gold". Yes, look at yourself as that desirable chest.

My mother in Jan. 2010 lost her last living sister. She was 87 years old. Several weeks before she died my mother made the trip to Greenburg, North Carolina to see her. While she was at the hospital she put the phone to her ear and let me talk to her. My mother said when I started talking to her she let out the biggest smile that you ever wanted to see. I didn't have the opportunity to meet my aunt Alberta until I was about 19 or 20 years of age. The first thing she did was try to help me out by setting me up in a beautiful house in Atlanta. Later she found out that I wasn't quite ready. Through the years our relationship grew stronger and stronger.

My family on my mother's side has this old tradition called "the little brown jug." It started with my grandmother (Agnes) full of Moonshine. My aunts Alberta, and Veal would always get together and go hunting for the little brown jug. Whatever the occasion, whether a funeral or family reunion, we would be together chasing that brown jug.

Our family came together because we had the same vision of bringing the family back together. They worked hard at this and it shows. My treasure is my family. God held a priceless treasure that would forever be in my heart and every time I turn around he's giving our family an increase. I quit drinking about 15 years ago, my aunts and my mother quite drinking several years ago, as well.

Their desires became more apparent toward God and they saw the same in me and depended on me to speak the word every time we came together. If I couldn't preach anywhere else I had a place at our family reunions. If I don't live another day God has made me rich in family and in Love. A loving wife and five wonderful children. "My cup runneth over."

After everything in life that could happen, my brother-in-law called me around July, 2010 to tell me that my nephew J.B. was in college in Tenn. And had given his life to Christ. J. B. had made this decision alone. He called me as a most proud father. A week later I received another called from my brother -in-law saying that J.B. was in an almost fatal accident and was in a coma in Tenn. Compound fractures of hands, the face, and brain stem damage. We didn't know if he would live. He did live through the grace of God and with a strong testimony, still praising God. I can see his mother and father coming closer to God through his courage and faith. J.B. went from an all-American athlete to now learning to walk again. He knows how to be patient and wait on the Lord.

Approximately the last of October or the first of November on a Friday morning, I got off from work and saw my family off to work and school. I got into bed with the intention to get up that evening to plan for a trip to Tampa with my family for the weekend. I was dosing off to sleep and must have been asleep for about an hour and a half to two hours. In my "dream state" I was saying that I need to go by the church and leave my offering. I wanted to work on my tithing (giving as God instructed in the Bible). A few minutes after my dreams or subconscious, the telephone rang. It was a call from my family in Tampa.

They told me that weekend was not a good weekend to bring my family down, but that was not the reason they called. They wanted to talk to me about something else. They said to me, you were talking about putting a below ground pool in with a screen enclosure a little while back. I said yes but my money was not right at the time and you were talking about putting one in at your home also. They said "yes but we called to talk about your pool, how much you think it cost. About 50 to 60 thousand?" I said "no not that much I've pricing them from 25 to35 thousand".

They said to me "well we want to put you a pool in", my heart dropped. Something I always wanted but was out of my reach at the time. God was holding this gift for me and my family. This gift was paid in full. My family in Tampa said to me "I didn't do this because you are family I did it because you are my friend". Again, it touched my heart and I couldn't hold back my tears. They said they called me that day because God put it on their heart and they didn't want to miss out on their blessing.

Giving to others, in need or just being obedient giving back to God. Remember you can't beat God giving. Let the way you live your life speak for you.

I don't know God's purpose for me, but he does so just trust, trust, trust, that he knows. I hope that this book helps keep you safe *In His Arms*. (We are our brother's keeper). How can I not love and forgive my brother?

I can look back almost 50 years ago, and say with confidence that God was there all the time carrying us 'In His Arms'.

Note: Being patient and obedient to God is the key to a wonderful life. All that I have seen in my life, Gods' presence has been my light and my strength. My mother celebrated her 90th birthday Dec. 10th 2010. It is now 2016 and this book will be released in January 2017...God willing and the creek don't rise, my mother will be here to share it with me.

"FOR I KNOW THE PLANS I HAVE FOR YOU," DECLARES THE LORD, "PLANS TO PROSPER YOU AND NOT TO HARM YOU, PLANS TO GIVE YOU HOPE AND A FUTURE." – JEREMIAH 29:11

MEMORIES

FIRE

Dayton Beach Fire Rescue

Bob Harman
 Bill Gilliland
  Tony Thompson

On the job...

Retirement...

Department Recognizes Black Firefighter

March 1 - 7, 2001

In celebration of Black History Month, the Daytona Beach Fire Department recognized one of its retired firefighters.

The department has recognized Anthony "Tony" Thompson, retired driver engineer, according to Lt. Gray Stone.

Thompson was born in Waycross, GA. He is married to Ruth Thompson. They have four children — three boys and one girl.

Thompson moved to Daytona Beach when he was 10 years old. After graduating high school, Thompson served several years in the United States Air Force. He returned to Daytona to serve his community.

Thompson started with the city in 1977 in the CETA Program as a maintenance worker for the police department. During this time, the city was recruiting firefighters under the same program.

Stone said the program opened doors for a lot of African-Americans. The program assisted cities with the hiring and training of minorities. Although it was set up as a temporary program, most cities

See FIREFIGHTER On Page 6B

Retired Daytona Beach firefighter Anthony "Tony" Thompson is saluted.

Firefighter —
Cont. from Page 1B

were able to hire these employees full-time at a later date.

Thompson in 1979 realized he had made a lifelong career in the fire service with the City of Daytona Beach. He said he felt this was going to be the way to help the community in which he had grown up.

In his dreams of helping people of the community, Thompson became one of three first African-American males to become paramedics in Volusia County. As Thompson worked with the city fire department, he was assigned to several special teams; water rescue, and the technical rescue team (high angle/confined space).

He was promoted to driver engineer, which required him to operate fire engines, rescue trucks, aerial equipment, and the department's fire boat.

In March of 2000, Thompson retired from the fire department where he had served 23 years. He became the first African-American to retire from the Daytona Beach Fire Department, Stone said.

His dream of working with children in the community still continues. He currently is working with the State Department of Juvenile Justice.

"Tony prides himself in helping our young citizens that have taken a wrong path in life," Stone said. "Tony uses his religion to give him strength, in helping steering these youths in the right direction. Tony is an avid singer and musician in his church, trying to spread his beliefs to the youths of our community.

"As a fellow worker, friend, and fire fighting brother, I salute, Anthony 'Tony' Thompson as the first African-American to retire from the Daytona Beach Fire Department. May God bless him and his family," Stone said.

The United States Air Force

Home Boys...
Tony Thompson & Julius Sessoms III

The Squad

FRIENDS & FAMILY

Mom & 3 of her Sisters

Mom's
Only bother
Johnny

Mom's
Sister - Alberta

My Sisters

Regina, Debra, Altamease & Brenda

Mom and the family

My Sons
Malcolm

Jonathan

My Sister...
Dr. Debra Sawyer

On Duty at all times...

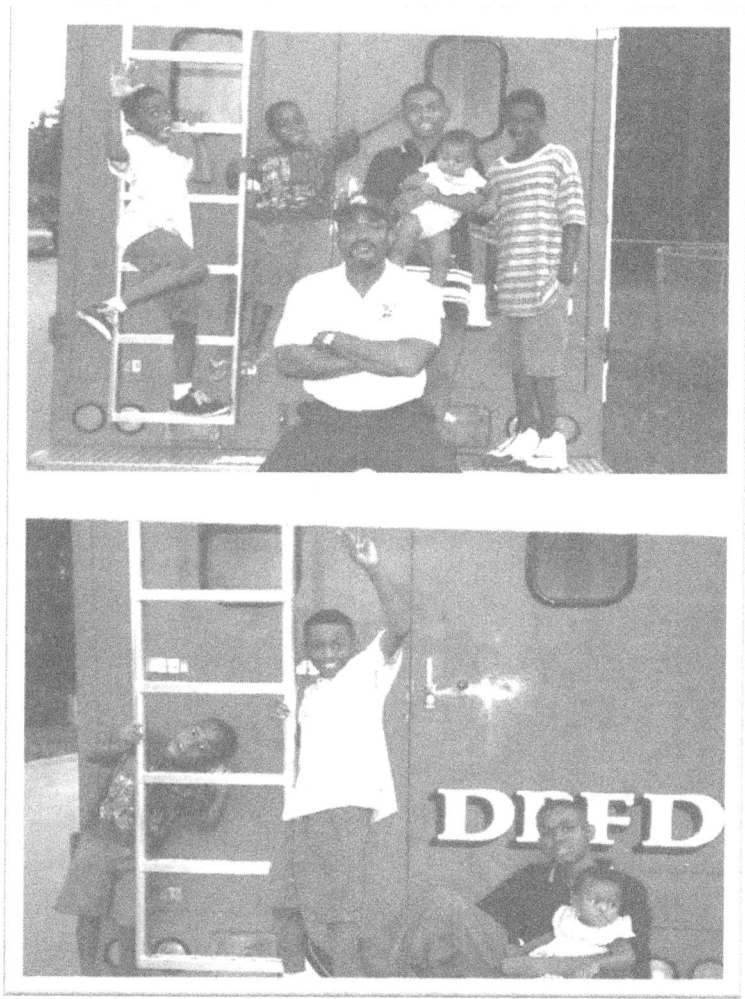

A Man and his family...

My Sons

Tony – Oldest Son

Marcus-Youngest Son

My Daughter...
Sherri

GRANDMOTHER AGNES (MATERNAL GRAND PARENT) AND AUNT VEAL
MATERNAL SIDE OF THE FAMILY

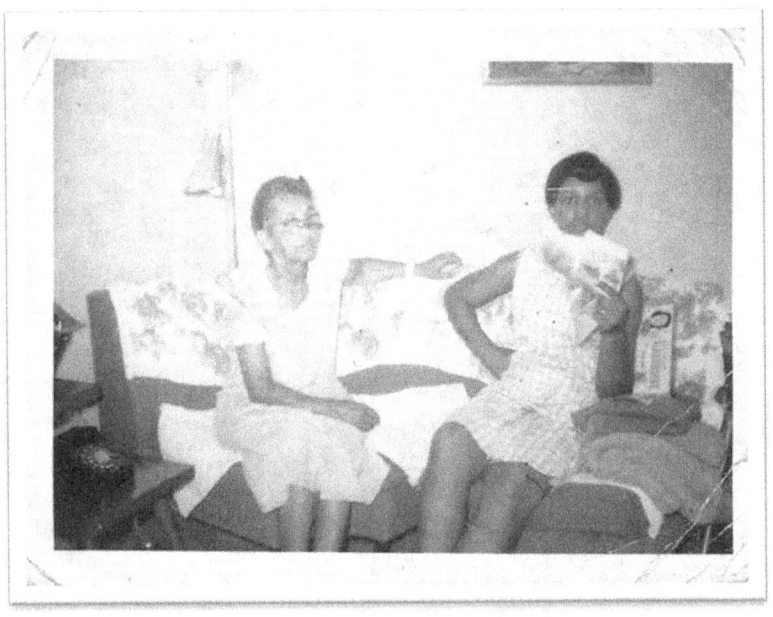

WE ARE FAMILY...

God and the love of Family is all I Need

Maternal Great - Grandparents

My Aunt Dora Lee

My Aunt Velvalene

Mom's baby sister

To God be the glory for the Great things that he has done!

www.ingramcontent.com/pod-product-compliance
Lightning Source LLC
Chambersburg PA
CBHW071621080526
44588CB00010B/1221